Pakistan:

A Legacy of the
Indian Khilafat Movement

Pakistan:

A Legacy of the
Indian Khilafat Movement

Husein Khimjee, Ph.D.

iUniverse LLC
Bloomington

Pakistan: A Legacy of the Indian Khilafat Movement

iUniverse books may be ordered through booksellers or by contacting:

iUniverse LLC
1663 Liberty Drive
Bloomington, IN 47403
www.iuniverse.com
1-800-Authors (1-800-288-4677)

ISBN: 978-1-4917-0207-9 (sc)
ISBN: 978-1-4917-0208-6 (ebk)

Printed in the United States of America

iUniverse rev. date: 08/28/2013

Contents

PREFACE

This book, *Pakistan: A Legacy of the Indian Khilafat Movement*, is a slightly revised version of the earlier work I did in the 1990's, *The Legacy of the Early Twentieth-Century Khilafat Movement in India*. In the aftermath of 9/11, I find this study even more interesting. Political and other events in Pakistan, since its inception in 1947, has shown that it has been struggling to live up to the ideology for what it was created: the ideology to be a nation where its `ulama (religious scholars) promote a true social justice, to be a nation at peace with all its citizens, to be a nation at peace with its neighbours and a nation that would reflect the era of Prophet Muhammad in Medina. There, in Medina, the Prophet established a truly pluralistic society in which all its citizens lived in peaceful co-existence with others. In Medina, under the famous "Constitution of Medina" the Prophet had presented, all citizens had full rights to express themselves freely and worship freely. In other words, a nation in which faith and reason went hand-in-hand, moderation always prevailed and extremism was considered hindrance to human progress. Extremism found no support. This is the model for which Pakistan was created. Such a model would have discouraged any other Muslim country or group to hijack the faith that abhors and condemns acts of violence; 9/11 and other acts of violence would not have occurred.

This book shows that the abolition of the institution of the Khilafat (Caliphate) in Turkey and the reasons given by the Turkish 'ulama (religious scholars) for its abolition, provided food for thought to the Muslim elite in India. Muslims saw in the reasons for this abolition a process of critical theological reasoning in which it was possible to update the institution of the Caliphate. This reflection made it possible for Muslims to demand, from the British government and the Indian National Congress, an Islamic state. This book argues that from such a development emerged the formation of a new country, the Islamic Republic of Pakistan. The carving out of a new country had all the blessings of the British government who drew the boundaries in the east and west of India giving birth to the new country. Hence, the title of this book, *Pakistan: A Legacy of the Khilafat Movement in India.*

The book discusses, with some evidence, how the Indian political leader, Muhammad Ali Jinnah (1876-1948), took up the challenge and used a three-pronged approach to sell the idea to the Muslim masses. After tracing earlier views of the Caliphate, this study looks at the connotations of the 'Ashura tragedy (the martyrdom of Imam al-Husayn, the grandson of Prophet Muhammad) in Karbala, which occurred in the year 61 A.H. (685 C.E.), and its commemoration every year, to show how recalling this event helped Jinnah in his Pakistan movement. The study shows that the khilafatist leaders were involved in using the event of the 'Ashura tragedy in Karbala to motivate Muslims. The study also presents writings and compositions of poems using the 'Ashura tragedy to arouse Muslims, literature recently released (1986) in the material proscribed by the British government in the 1920's and 1930's.

Finally, the study shows that in the thinking of twentieth-century Indian Muslims, the institutional rationale of the Caliphate seems to have evolved, from a one-man Caliph-emperor to a socially elected, democratic caliphate state, from the idea of an individual Caliph to the concept of an Islamic state.

One difficulty in thinking about writing this book has been that although the Khilafat movement in early twentieth century

India was a movement of faith, it was also a movement in history. How can one separate the two and yet do proper justice to the topic in a book written, not for any religious institutions but for secular readership, and for students in western universities? It was only the exceptional support and encouragement of my dear friend and professor, the late Dr. Willard G. Oxtoby, who told me to "forge ahead and write" the thesis when I first discussed with him in 1990's. I am equally grateful to Dr. Naren K. Wagle for his most valuable suggestions and criticisms which enabled me to strengthen my ideas. Dr. Wagle's expertise in the area and his ability to analyze the historical events of the period rendered immense help in the final stages of my earlier thinking and initial writing on this subject. My thanks also go to Dr. Sheila McDonough, Professor Milton Israel and Professor Joseph O'Connell, for reading my original work in the 1990's on this subject and for giving me helpful hints. This book is only a slightly revised version of that.

The Proscribed Material in my earlier work was perhaps used for the very first time in research on the subject. Some of this material was gathered during research visits to the India Office of the British Library in London. My thanks are due to the librarians there who helped me locate some of the materials I have also used in this book. My grateful thanks also go to Mr. Parry Hall of the University of Toronto, who was extremely helpful each time I approached him during my research.

Among many individuals who have also helped me is Professor Mahmoud Ayoub who alerted me early in my thinking to some interesting dimensions. Another person with whom I had an interesting discussion was Mr. Rafi Khan, who lived through the days of the Pakistan movement. It was, therefore, fascinating to speak with him. Mr.Khan read my Proscribed Material with interest and gave valuable suggestions. His assistance with some Urdu sources and their translation was very helpful.

For this particular book, I am thankful also to Mr. Sakir Jetha and to my publisher's Check-in Coordinator, Mr. Barry Lee. Sakir helped me convert some of my PDF files into manageable Word format. Barry was professional in handling my Manuscript and made sure there was no undue delay in moving it forward to the publication stage.

Finally, my thanks go to all my family members, who have never stopped encouraging me. Most importantly, my deepest thanks go to Kaniz, my wife, my daughter Fehmida, my son-in-law Yousuf and my grandchildren Maryam, Ismail and Fatima. It is to them I dedicate this book.

CHAPTER ONE:
INTRODUCTION TO THE KHILAFAT MOVEMENT

A unique phenomenon in major Islamic reform movements has been that they endeavored to create for Muslims an environment of *raja'a*[1]. In this regard, the appeal from the leaders of movement has always been religious in tone. The content of their appeal has always been to reform the society and return to the basic faith in which there is a unanimous acceptance of the period of the Prophet. This period, and the one that followed it, to the end of the *Khulafa al-Rashidun*[2], a period of about half a century from the advent of the Prophet (610-661 C.E.); provide for Muslims a model of how they, and the Islamic society in which they live, should function. The ideal state to which Muslim movements have endeavored to appeal is a state in which there is a struggle[3] to be 'born again into the

---

[1] *Raja*' is an Arabic word meaning 'to return'. In this context, it would mean to return to the pristine days of the ideal Islamic society. For Muslims, this is in the period of The Prophet where true social justice prevailed as people of all faiths and races lived in peaceful co-existence.

[2] *Khulafa al-Rashidun* or the 'Rightly Guided Caliphs' refers to the period of the rule of the first four Caliphs after the passing away of The Prophet.

[3] The word 'struggle' is translated in Arabic as *jihad*. The literal meaning of *jihad* is 'struggle, exertion'. In the context of reforming the society, *jihad* has two levels. At an individual level, it is called *jihad al-Akbar* (the greatest struggle). At this level, there is a denial of any indulgence considered illegitimate in Islam. At a societal level, it would be jihad *al-Asghar* (the smallest struggle), in which the society as a whole has to endeavor to bring about

life in which one avoids the state of forgetfulness that the true Sovereign Lord is only Allah[4]. Further, He is the only One to be worshipped and therefore, His laws are the only laws that are supreme and must be obeyed. He has the total authority which is not corrupt, since in His attributes He is shown as *al-`Azizu al-Hakim* (The Mighty the Wise). He is the Just Allah. Muslims feel therefore, a very

> "Deep religious anger at the kind of society in which they themselves live; societies dominated by callousness and pride of the unjustly rich who squander wealth and oppress the weak. The modern period of colonial and neocolonial dependency, which has typically been seen to benefit Europeans and their collaborators, has thus proven fertile ground for renewal and revolt . . ."[5]

From the last days of the Mughal emperor Akbar (seventeenth century) down to the modern period (twentieth century), Muslims in India produced diversity of Islamic movements. All the movements are seen to have the straits described above, albeit in varying degrees.

The Khilafat movement in the early twentieth century had the same ingredients. It also had in it a pan-Indian content

---

legitimate political and social reforms. For a comprehensive explanation See also John Esposito, *Islam: The Straight Path,* (New York: Oxford University Press, 2011), pp.113-4; Karen Armstrong, *Muhammad: A Biography of The Prophet,* (San Francisco: Harprer Collins, 1993), pp.168-180.

[4] Allah is simply an Arabic name for God. Allah meaning God is not unique to Islam and has been in use for centuries before the advent of Islam. People of all faiths in Arabic speaking world use Allah when they refer to God. See also Khimjee, Husein, *The Attributes of God in the Monotheistic Faiths of Judeo-Christian and Islamic Traditions,*(Bloomington:iUniverse, 2011), pp.1-7.

[5] Barbara Daly Metcalf, *Islamc Revival in British India: Deoband, 1860-1900* (Princeton: Princeton University Press, 1892), pp. 4-5.

because after the 1857 uprisings, Muslims found themselves stripped of much that belonged to their Islamic culture in India. They also found themselves in increasing competition with Hindus and other non-Muslims. But at the heart of the Khilafat movement was the idea of preservation of that ideal Islamic symbol, the Caliphate that had the duty to create and defend an environment of the uncorrupted community in the time of the Prophet.

Since it was held that there would be no more Prophets, the majority Sunni Muslims came to believe that authority rested upon the Caliph, the successor to the Prophet Muhammad. The caliph's role would be to ensure the prevailing of divine justice on the earth. The caliph, therefore, was both the spiritual and the temporal ruler.

"It is of the essence of Sunni doctrine that the *umma*, the historic community, is based upon the Sharia, that its historical development is divinely guided, and its continuity guaranteed by the infallible authority of ijma. Therefore, the jurists, as keepers of the public conscience, had a duty to demonstrate afresh for each generation the legality of its political constitution. This question was in their vie bound up with that of the caliphate, which, as an institution, is essentially the symbol of the supremacy of Sharia"[6].

The Khilafat movement in India in the early part of the twentieth century was an attempt to save this Islamic symbol from collapse. Muslims in India looked up to the institution of caliphate as the prevailing Islamic symbol, the shadow of God on earth. During the Mughal period, the Mughal emperors had appropriated in India the title of Khalifa (Caliph) for themselves. This notion of the caliphate was ingrained in their

---

[6] See Hamilton A. R. Gibb, ed. Stanford J. Shaw and William R. Polk, *Studies on the Civilization of Islam* (Toronto: S. J. Reginald Saunders and Co., 1962), p. 141.

psyche ever since the first Muslims set foot in India, as we shall see in the following paragraphs.

With the collapse of the Ottoman empire at the end of World War I in 1919, the victorious British empire and the European powers were about to sign the peace treaty that would divide the Ottoman lands. The temporal and spiritual authority of the cherished caliphate, the symbol of Islam, would vanish. In some ways, many Muslims in India also felt that they were accessories to the Ottoman defeat. They had sided with the British government and its allied forces to fight against the army of their caliph. This had to be redeemed by saving the whole institution of the caliphate from collapse. But more than that, Muslims were always in the minority in India. With the collapse of the caliphate, they would be left orphans, at the mercy of the ruling British, in the milieu of a Hindu majority. In this regard, the Muslim Khilafatist leaders drew a clear distinction in their minds. When it came to describing their beliefs, they showed that they were Muslims with clearly extra-territorial loyalties. When it came to describing themselves and the politics they were dealing with, they clearly thought in the Indian terms. Muhammad Ali, for instance, had said that when it came to his Islamic beliefs, he was and he is and will always be a Muslim. But when it came to India and its future, he was an Indian first, an Indian last and nothing but an Indian. It is noteworthy that even those Muslim leaders who championed the *muttahidah qawmiyyah* (the one-nation theory) were fully afflicted with this notion[7]

This book is an attempt, therefore, to reconstruct the ideology and nationality of Muslims of India during the Khilafat movement and its aftermath.

---

[7] See Rizwan Malik, *Mawlana Husayn Madani and Jam`iyat `ulama-i-Hind 1920-1957: Status of Islam and Muslims in India,* Thesis, University of Toronto, 1955, pp. 98ff.

There have been some interesting published dissertations from western scholars specifically dealing with the subject of the Khilafat movement in India in the early twentieth century. Their writings on the Khilafat movement have tended to explain Muslim nationalism in the Indian subcontinent in the light of essentially a pan Islamic Khilafat issue.

This book, without undermining the Indian nationalism in the Indian subcontinent, examines in depth the Indian Muslims' religious ethos which sustained their Islamic identity in India. The aspect of Indian nationalism mentioned by other scholars only reinforced their Islamic identity.'

In an early thesis on the Khilafat movements William Watson stresses psychological support the movement offered to Muslims so that they could participate in the majority Hindu national movement; and repudiate their loyalty to Britain. Watson tells us that the Khilafat movement ended without accomplishing anything that it set out to do. The basic intention of Indian Muslims, as Watson sees it, was to bring about a world in which Indian Muslims could live Islamically as Indians. One opportunity accorded them, in this regard, was unity with Hindus in Gandhi's non-co-operation movement. At the level of expediency it was absolutely vital for Muslims to co-operate fully with Hindus to attain their objective. Both Hindus and Muslims were aware that the only valid argument the British government had for their continuing subjugation of India was that Hindus and Muslims could never unite and that therefore the British government's withdrawal would leave a situation of an open warfare. From Gandhi's Indian nationalist viewpoint, a clear proof of unity with Muslims had to be provided to support the Muslims in a specific Islamic issue. But although realistic in their communal concerns and co-operative action on the part of the India as a whole, the Khilafat movement itself was hopelessly far from realism. For in the world situation of the 1920's how could the British government, Watson wonders, allow preservation of the boundaries of the Ottoman empire demanded by Muslims as they were in 1914? The realities of the 1920's were very different. The Ottoman empire had been defeated with its allies, and the western powers had divided its territories. Moreover, the Arabs were already seeking independence from the Ottoman Turks, and the Turks were themselves shying away from their imperial past and were demanding their own constitution. Moreover, the world's Muslims' sentiments were not united with Indian Muslims on the issue of preserving an Ottoman emperor as the Caliph for all Muslims. The Middle Easterners were occupied with their own problems of nationalism. Also, British policies vis-a-vis the Ottoman empire had been reversed. The treaties made with allies during war years had required of them to divide the Ottoman lands. The Khilafat demand to set the clock back to 1914 just would not make any sense. Watson dismisses the movement as unrealistic given the world situation of the time. The perplexity Watson shows about the movement is quite understandable. Clearly, he does not see how the institution of the Caliphate domiciled in Turkey, defeated by the world powers, would benefit the future of Muslims domiciled in the India of the 1920's. Instead, Muslims should have made it their priority to continue to foster and build unity with Hindus to achieve their goal. Watson concludes: If Indians had been able to see any positive accomplishments resulting from their efforts, they probably would have worked on in unity . . . probably then Indian Muslims would have discovered that the continued existence of the Khilafah was not a pre requisite to their ability to live Islamically as Indians[8].

A.C. Niemeijer, in his dissertation on the Khilafat movement emphasizes on its pan-Islamic content and suggests that the Khilafat movement in India was a monolithic Indo-Muslim response to the fate of the caliphate. Niemeijer writes his thesis based on the theories of nationalism and suggests that the whole notion of pan-Islamism in the Khilafat movement meant that the movement started on the wrong foot. Had it shunned

---

[8]   Ibid., p.86.

the idea of Pan—Islamism, it might have succeeded in forming for the Indian Muslims some kind of Muslim nationalism[9].

Gail Minault, another scholar on the Khilafat movement[10] in India, picks up from where Watson left off. She argues that the mere pan-Islamic content in the Khilafat movement described by scholars is neither adequate nor simple to interpret. It shows extra-territorial loyalty and implies that Indians were not truly supportive of Indian nationalism in their hearts. In describing pan-Islamic sentiments these scholars neglected the most significant aspects of the movement. That is, they neglected the process of communication going on in India at the time of the Khilafat movement at various levels in the society. There were new methods of organizing political activity which were tried, and also, the styles of religious and political leadership were changing. Minault looks into the movement using some Urdu sources to show that it used pan-Islamic symbols to fuse a pan-Indian Muslim constituency. To her, the relevance of the movement was that it endeavored to reconcile Islamic identity with Indian nationality. The movement was a quest to forge a pan-Indian Islam:

> A united, pan-Indian Islam constituency, if it could in fact be mobilized, would in turn permit genuine Muslim participation in the Indian nationalist movement. (It) . . . could offset their minority status by their ability to bargain from the position of strength whether with the British government or with the Hindus of the Indian National Congress' [11]

She finds that the Khilafat movement did not succeed in uniting the Indian Muslims politically and in forging a

---

[9]   see A.C. Niemeijer, *The Khilafat Movement in India* 1919-1924, (The Hague: Martinus Nijhoff, 1972), pp. 22-48, 164-178.

[10]   "Gail Minault, The Khilafat *Movement: Religious Symbolism and Political Mobilization in* India (New York Columbia University Press), 1982.

[11]   Minault., pp. 2-3.

permanent Hindu-Muslim nationalist alliance. Neither did it succeed in preserving the Caliphate.

My book argues that the collapse of the Khilafat movement was not the end of the whole issue of the Caliphate. Muslims remained committed to this symbol as a representative of the Prophet on this earth. In other words, Muslims showed to define their corporate existence out of their own religious sentiments. They gave their politics a religious legitimacy based upon the classical framework of Islamic thinking. This was embodied in the institution of the Caliphate and the necessity of its existence, explained in the middle ages in the writings of al-Mawardi, as we shall see later.

In developing my argument, I shall be relying on a body of source material referred to here as the "Proscribed Materials". The British government in India had proscribed certain printed material from circulation for four decades (1910's to 1940's). Books, pamphlets, periodicals, newspapers, handbills and even some posters that were proscribed by the British government were accumulated in London in the library of the India Office and in the British Museum library. These collections were closed to the public, simply locked away in their original wrappings. They were neither sorted out nor listed. The reason given for their proscription was that they promoted criticism of the British administration in India and promoted racial strife. The first permanent press control was laid down in India by virtue of the Indian Press Act of 1867. The interpretation of the Act of showed what constituted the seditious material. It was widened in 1898. It embraced anything which attempted to bring or excite dissatisfaction to the British government in India. By the turn of the century two main categories of Proscribed Material was established: criticism of the British colonial government coupled with increasing demand for self-government, and expressions of communal conflict which would excite inter-communal and interreligious conflict. After the partition of Bengal in 1905, the growing revolutionary activity brought about the Indian Press Act of 1910. This provided a legal base for proscription of what was considered to be "seditious material", whether home produced or originating from abroad. The Act provided machinery to close down presses and publishers of seditious material jailed.

After the First World War, in response to the Rowlatt Act, Gandhi united his non-cooperation movement with the Indian Muslims Khilafat movement. At this time, there were Khilafat movement propagandists in Turkey. Material issued by them was proscribed. The tragedy of Jalianwalla Bagh in 1919 promoted anti-government poetry. After the collapse of the Khilafat movement, communal tensions were responsible for more poetry considered seditious by the British government. During this period and shortly afterwards as the Pakistan movement was gathering momentum, poems invoking Karbala's `Ashura tragedy also appeared. These poems were in response to the Hindu attack upon Muslims during the 'Ashura treagedy commemoration of Imam al-Husayn. When the publication was proscribed, all copies were to be destroyed except five. Three copies were kept by the Keeper of Records in New Delhi (now National Archives of India). The other two copies were sent to London. Until 1968 these were closed to the public. The micro-fiche edition is very recent. It contains most, but not all, of the catalogued items in London office[12].

The collapse of the Khilafat movement left a legacy for Muslims of India upon which they built new structures. These structures enabled them to create an edifice that would preserve the symbol of Caliphate in the form of a *jama'a,* a community. The legacy of the movement remained with Muslim intellectuals and leaders like Muhammad Iqbal, Maulana Abul Kalam Azad and even other lesser known Muslims throughout the period leading to Partition, as we see in the writings

---

[12]   Publications Proscribed by the Government of India (London, 1985) pp. viiiff. Also see Banned: Controversial Literature and Political Control in India, 1907-1947 (New York: Columbia University Press, 1974).

expressed in the Proscribed Material. The Proscribed Material, used for the first time in this thesis, shows that as late as 1940's, scholars and other lesser known Muslims were writing literature and composing poems on the glory of the Caliphate. The net result of the Khilafat movement was that it showed Muslims ways to mobilize the masses and create public support. It showed how to rally public support through fund-raising and membership drives, through publication of pamphlets and journals, through *khutbas* (sermons) in the mosques and through publications of *sha'iris* (poems, verses). After the collapse of the Khilafat movement as Muslims continued to remain mobilized, this time to assist in their separateness from non-Muslims as an um*ma* (one community) despite the vast divergence found among the Indian population. The Proscribed Material shows that from 1920 to 1940, the issue of Islamic unity which started with the Khilafat issue in 1919 never died down in the psyche of Indian Muslims. The urge to restore the Caliphate arose, using the symbol of `*Ashura* tragedy at Karbala and the martyrdom of Imam al-Husayn, itself a Khilafat issue. In its wake, as Muslims became united in this issue, it transcended their Shi'a-Sunni divide. In the post-Khilafat period, Indian Muslims are shown to have expressed their resentments against their economic exploitation by non-Muslims.

To counteract this, Muslims took certain steps and used the Khilafat symbol to discard the local culture as they are urged to go back to Islam.

Furthermore, as a general background to the Khilafat movement, this book also outlines the history of Muslims in the sub-continent from the earliest time, when a part of India was incorporated into the Umayyad and later the Abbasid caliphate, until the recent times. In the whole of this period, we find a persistent theme, or a common thread that binds the Muslim history despite the divergences over time. It is argued in this book that this common thread is the persistent longing of Muslims in India as a corporate entity to associate with, or be part of, the larger corporate entity of Muslims outside India, if only expressed in the theory of the Caliphate. The concept of the necessity of the Caliph was ingrained in their corporate psyche.

Muslims are seen arriving in India for the first time during the expansion period of the early caliphate. Thus, al-Baladhuri, in his *Futuh al-Buldan*[13] tells us that from the earliest times the attempt to conquer India for Muslims was made under the names of caliphs in Madina. The first Muslim attempt at the conquest of India occurred as early as the period of the second Caliph of Islam, Umar ibn al-Khattab (634-644). Although the campaign was not very successful[14], the intelligence-gathering activities continued throughout the period of the "the *Khulafa al-Rashidun.* In the time of 'Ali (656-661) there was a small incursion upon Sind in 660. Under the Umayyad Walid ibn Abd al-Malik al-Hajjaj ibn Yusuf[15], the governor of Iraq sent a well-organized Arab expedition under Muhammad bin Qassim in 711. Muhammad bin Qassim conquered Sind in the name of the Umayyad Caliph and made the conquest of India a goal of the Umayyad caliphate. Sind remained part of the Umayyads throughout the Umayyad dynasty. After their overthrow in 750, it remained part of the Abbasid caliphate and became culturally integrated as part of *Dar al-Islam.* Later, the Abbasid caliph al Mu'tamid bestowed Sind in 871 to a Saffarid prince, Ya'qub ibn

---

[13] See Ahmed ibn Yahya ibn jabir al Baladhuri, *Kitab Futuh al-Buldan* (Cairo, 1932), pp. 419ff.

[14] The campaign was led by Abull 'As Mughira. It was not very successful because there was no clear consensus as to the plan of land invasion. See Mirza Kalichbeg Fredunbeg, *The Chachnamah, An Ancient History of Sind*, pp.57 ff.

[15] We are told that in plan of al-Hajjaj's conquests, the plan was to conquer the whole of the north and south of Central Asia and connect it with China. Although this did not happen, in the same year 711, there were conquests for the Umayyad caliphate in North Africa and Spain.

Layth, who became virtual ruler from the Indus Valley in the south to Tukharistan in the north.

The Friday *khutba*s (sermons) in the mosques continued to mention the names of Abbasid caliphs[16]. After subjugation under several Muslim dynasties, Sind eventually adopted the theory of Khilafat as presented by al-Mawardi[17]. The ruler accepted temporal authority to rule over the state but recognized the spiritual authority of the Caliph in Baghdad. Erwin Rosenthal tells us that "this may be nothing more than a legal fiction; but it alone guaranteed the unity of Islam under the overall authority of Shari'a[18].

When Mahmud of Ghazna invaded north western India in 1014, and made Lahore his dynasty's first outpost in 1030, he crystallized this concept of the caliphate. Once again, Mahmud of Ghazna's perception of a universal caliph made the Caliph in Baghdad a symbol of association that "bound Muslim India to the Muslim world[19].

---

[16] When the Saffarids power collapsed, Sind passed through several other dynasties including Hindus until the Fatimid Shi`as took it in 883 C.E. The Fatimids paid their allegiance to the Fatimid caliphs in Cairo. The practice of mentioning names of caliphs (this time, the Fatimid caliphs in Cairo) continued. Muslims under Islamic rule in India had already accepted the symbol and grandeur of the institution of caliphate even then.

[17] Further on Mawardi's theory is discussed later in this chapter. See al-Mawardi, *al-Ahkam al-Sul taniyya,* Cairo, 1881. See also H.A.R. Gibb, in "Al-Mawardi's Theory of Khilafah" in Islamic Culture (1937), xi, 3, pp. 291-302.

[18] See Erwin I. J. Rosenthal, *Political Thought in Mediaeval Islam*, Cambridge, 1958.

[19] See Aziz Ahmad, *Studies in Islamic Culture in the Indian Environment,* p. 5.

The Ghaznavid Sultans continued for several succeeding generations to receive the Khilafat investiture[20].

The Ghurids[21], who sacked the Ghaznavids, and their successors, the Delhi Sultans, continued in the tradition of considering themselves and instilling in the minds of their Indian subjects that they (the rulers) were the vassals of the Abbasid caliphs. The situation changed only after the demise of the Abbasids at the hands of the Mongols in 1258. The ruling Khalji dynasty (1290-1320) in India reconciled itself to the idea of a universal caliph in the abstract; referring to themselves with titles like *nasir-al-amir al-Mu'minin* (helpers of the leader of believers) or *yamin al-khilafat* (the right hand of the universal caliph). Interestingly, the last ruler of the Khalji dynasty, Qutb al-Din Mubarak (1316-1320), gave himself the actual title of the Abbasid caliph al-Wathiq and also called himself by the caliphal titles of *Amir al-Mu'minin* and *al-imam al-A'zam*.

The Tughluq dynasty (1320-1413, successors to the Khalji dynasty) returned to the hypothesis of a "universal" caliphate. We are told that if one is permitted to apply a modem term to the medieval religio-political idealism in Muhammad bin Tughluq, he can also be described as the first pan-Islamist in India, who believed in the world of Islam as a composite totality, at the center of which was the authority of Abbasid caliph[22].

---

[20] Mahmud Ghaznavils coins bore the name of Abbasid caliphs together with this own name. This practice continued by his successors at Ghazna and Lahore. See "Coins of the Kings of Ghazni", Journal of the Royal Asiatic Society, IX, 267 ; xvii, 138.

[21] The Ghaznavids were succeeded by the Ghurid, Iltemish (slaves) and the Khalji dynasties. Their coins, too, carried the name of the Abbasid Caliph. In the time of the Gnurid Sultan, Muiz al-Din Muhammad ibn Sam Ghuri (r. 1174 1206), his name appeared together with the Abbasid Caliph. Ibid., p. 138.

[22] See Ahmad, p.8.

Muhammad bin Tughluq sought investiture from the Abbasid caliph, now in Cairo. Interestingly, when his successor Firoz Shah Tughluq received his investiture from the Abbasid caliph, he referred the caliph as follows:

"The greatest and best of honours that I obtained through God's mercy was, that by my obedience and piety, and friendliness and submission to khalifa, the representative of the Holy Prophet, my authority was confirmed; for it is by his sanction that the power of king is assured, and no king is secure until he has submitted himself to the khalifa and has received a confirmation from the sacred throne . . . confirming my authority as deputy of the khalifa . . ."[23]

If any period provided a lull in the notion that the universal caliphate lay only with the Ottomans in the person of their Sultans, it was the period of the Mughal emperor[24] Akbar who

---

[23] See Hafeez Malik, *Moslem Nationalism in India and Pakistan*, (Washington: Public Affairs Press, 1963), p. 19.

[24] The Mughal empire was founded in 1526 by a Chaghatai Turkish ruler, Zahir al-Din Muhammad Babur (r.1526-1530). Babur defeated the last Sultan of the Delhi Sultanate, Ibrahim Lodi, at the battle of Panipat. After occupying Delhi, he moved his capital to Agra. Despite large scale conversions to Islam and immigration, Islam always remained a minority in India. When Akbar came to power in 1556, he was presiding over a predominantly non-Muslim society. Akbar himself was a Muslim following the the teachings of a great Sufi shaykh, Salim Chishty (d. 1571). In Akbar's reign, the religious climate was more open and tolerant towards others. Centuries of Muslim rule had brought about sympathetic co-existence, as mystics, scholars and saints were seeking some form of synthesis. In 16th century, as Akbar's piety seemed to be declining, conflict arose between him and the 'ulama of the court. The 'ulama wanted him to display his piety and devotion to Islam openly so that he could be a model for others to follow. The 'ulama also wanted Akbar to strictly conform to the Islamic Shari'a and most importantly, to make his empire a model for *Dar al-Islam*.

ruled India from 1556-1605[25] and his successors, down to Aurangzeb (1658-1707). But the situation changed radically after the death of Aurangzeb. The Ottomans soon laid their claims of the caliphate of the whole of *Dar al-Islam*. Muslims in India had no objection. In their minds, as already explained earlier, the legitimacy of one caliph for the entire Muslim world was already ingrained. We are told that this deeply rooted belief in the institution of the caliphate as a symbol, had a two-pronged impact on Indian Muslims. As Hafiz Malik aptly observes:

"From the rule of Muhammad ibn-al-Qasim to that of the British they considered themselves part of the larger brotherhood of Islam. This entailed an extra-territorial allegiance which retarded the development of a territorially centered secular nationalism . . . At the same time it precluded Hindu-Muslim cooperation, a pre-requisite for the creation of a joint Hindu-Muslim nationality"[26].

Linked with this was also the issue of jobs and grants theologians and jurists had become accustomed to. In the years 1578-1579, Akbar decided to bring about sweeping reforms in which he made pious land grants available to learned men of all religions, not just the 'ulama. Akbar also abolished the practice of jizya. The 'ulama were bitterly opposed to these reforms. Finally, in 1579, Akbar issued an edict that he would be the chief arbiter for all religious affairs. The royal edict also claimed Akbar to be the Caliph in preference to the Ottoman Sultan-emperor, who had claimed that title since seizing control of the Holy cities in 1517.

[25] It is noteworthy to mention, though, that when Akbar became an emperor at the death of his father in 1556, one of the first things that he did was to send a letter to the Ottoman emperor Sulayman the Magnificent in which he addressed him as 'the Khalif on earth, a refuge of princes of the time, and adjuster of the lords of the age'. See Ahmad, p. 25.

[26] 'See Malik, p. 21.

It is noteworthy that even the rejection of Mughal emperor Akbar and some of his successors in the Mughal empire not to recognize the Ottoman caliph was never to replace the caliph with their authority. Historical accounts tell us that although

> "Akbar and other powerful Moghul sovereigns assumed the title of Caliph, their claims never encompassed the whole Muslim world; they wanted only to convince their Muslim subjects in India that no outside authority existed which was legitimate and powerful enough to sanction their rule"[27].

But besides this, there were two movements that are shown to have influenced his mind. One was the *Alfi*[28] movement. This movement claimed that since it was a thousand years since the advent of the Prophet, the time was ripe for the advent of a rejuvenator or renewer of the faith. This rejuvenator would have an authority of an Imam in the community. Since Akbar was already going through a spiritual crisis, we are told that some of the `ulama-i-su' (the evil scholars), who were close to Akbar found an opportunity, and

> ". . . they showed falsehood in the form of truth, and evil in the garb of good, bewildering a monarch . . . (so that) . . . doubts accumulated in his mind and matters got out of control. The strong defenses of the revealed law broke down; and after five or six years hardly any trace of Islam was left in him"[29].

The second movement was the *Mahdi* movement. Their claim was reformism and liberalism in religion. Some from the `ulama-i-su' took opportunity to put ideas into his mind. As a

---

27   See Malik, p. 21.

28   *Alf* is an Arabic word denoting a number thousand. There are traditions cited in which the Prophet is reported to have said that every millenium there would be a reformer in the community who will rejuvenate the ummah.

29   See Ahmad, p. 69.

result, by 1578, Akbar was seen passing through spiritual crisis and shifted from orthodoxy to generalized eclecticism. Within three years after that he promulgated his *din-i-ilahi*. Shaykh Ahmad Sirhindi, commenting on this period in the life of Indian Muslims said that "Every evil that appeared in those days . . . was due to the wickedness of these evil *'ulama* who have been a menace to mankind and to the Word of God". But not all the so called "evil scholars" were in fact evil. During the last years of Akbar's reign, and continuously throughout the eighteenth and the nineteenth centuries there arose movements from the concerned *'ulama*. Their concern was clearly to save from the fall Indian Muslim political power and patronage of Muslim religion and culture. It is necessary that we make here at least a brief mention of the major movements. It was through these movements and the influence of the *'ulama* that were behind it that Muslims became rejuvenated. Akbar's din-*i-ilahi* did not succeed.

The Naqshabandi order was a Sufi order. It arose directly as a result of Akbar's eclecticism. The Naqshabandiyah was an orthodox movement and gained momentum during last years of Akbar's reign in the personality of one Khwaja Baqi billah. Its flowering is seen in his disciple, Shaykh Ahmad Sirhindi (1564-1624). The scholarly writings of Sirhindi earned him a position to assist the wazir Abu al-Fazl at Akbar's court to assist him in his literary work. Later he devoted himself fully to the cause of reform. Sirhindi wrote several treatises and letters. In the literature dealing with (the) history of Islam in India, we are told by scholars the prestige Sirhindi was holding. We are told by Yohanan Friedman that:

"Sirhindi holds a very special position. His disciples gave him the honorific title of the Renewer of the Second Millennium (*mujaddid-i-alf-i thani*). His celebrated collection of letters, which came to be known as *Maktubat-i Imam-Rabbani*, was repeatedly hailed as a landmark in the development of Muslim religious thought in India . . . Sirhindi brought about major changes in the development of Islam in the subcontinent . . . (and) . . . reversed the heretical trends of the period of Akbar and restored the pristine purity of Islam."[30].

For a time, Sirhindi was also a disciple of the Chishti, Suharwardi and *Qadi*ri orders but chose the Naqshabandi because its simplicity in meeting the challenges of the contemporary heresies. Sirhindi took up the task of restoring in Indian Islam the prestige of the Prophet which seemed weakened by the *Alfi* movement and at the hints that Akbar's status was near prophetic. Sirhindi refuted these claims in his first work, *Ithbat-I Nabuwwat* and followed up with letters he wrote to individuals in which he totally denounced Akbar's heresy. When Akbar died and his son Jahangir came to the throne in 1605, Sirhindi advised his disciples in court to guide the new emperor correctly and save him from falling into the hands of the *'ulama-i Su'*. Within Islam, Sirhindi's endeavors were to close the breach between the *shari'a* and the *tariqa*[31].

Sirhindi' s reform tactics[32], and his call of 'back to basics,' had far-reaching consequences. Muslims became radically

---

[30]   'See Yohanan Friedman, *Shaykh Ahmad Sirhindi: An Outline of His Thought and a Study of His Image in the Eyes of Posterity* (Montreal: McGill University Institute of Islamic Studies, 1971) p. xiii. See also Encyclopaedia Iranica, http://www.iranicaonline. org/articles/ahmad-serhendi-shaikh-outstanding-mughal-m ystic-and-prolific-writer-on-sufi-themes

[31]   See Ahmad, pp.183ff.

[32]   Sirhindi trained several disciples for the Islamic propagation he called ittiba--i sunna (back to following the ways of the Prophet). These disciples were sent through out the Muslim empire. Sirhindi followed up with letters to several individuals throughout the Islamic empire laying emphasis on the ittiba'-I sunna. Sirhindi also managed to penetrate the Mughal army and extract a vow from all Muslims that they would not obey any law contradictory to Islam. Much later, in the twentieth century, Iqbal expresses in one of his poems feeling of gratitude for his services in the cause of Allah.

affected, opposed secularization of Muslim rule in India, and set in motion those forces for the re-creation of the pre-War political system which triumphed during the reign of Jahangir's grandson, Emperor Aurangzeb). But by the middle of the 18th century, after the death of Aurangzeb in 1707, India suffered external invasions[33] and uprising from within the Mughal empire."[34] On the other hand, the British East India Company was continuing to gain ground and extend its authority in India. As the Company saw the Mughal empire weakening, it forged alliances with local rulers whom the Mughals had set up. By 1765, the East India company had extended its influence and control so much that it acquired the rights to collect the revenue in Bengal. This development has been discussed as one of the earliest, and one of the most drastic, examples European exploitation of Muslim power. Following this, the East India Company, continued to exploit the situation in India. By the nineteenth century, when the indigenous rule in India had ended, there were already substantial changes in the land. Also, the Western industrialized economy was being introduced in India. It was the *'ulama* who began to respond to this situation[35]. Influenced by the Naqshabandi Sufi order, the *'ulama*, particularly of the imperial court of Delhi, began to reassert themselves in order to set a synthetic and unified standard of correct religious belief and practice[36]. Any action they took was independent, since the Mughal emperors were too weak to give the *'ulama* any organized support. In doing so, the *'ulama* showed their striking note of religious commitment

---

Iqbal points out in his poem that it was Allah who alerted Sirhindi to the dangers that wereinherent in Akbar's religious and political declaration in Din-I I l a h i. See Malik, pp. 54-55.

[33] Ibid., p.55

[34] Invasion from Persia by Nadir Shah (r. 1736-1747) and successive Afghani attacks by Abdali (r.1747-1773) in 1748, 1757,1760.

[35] Among the pre-1857 'ulama who responded was Shah Waliyullah Dahlavi. See Metcalf, pp. 35-43.

[36] Metcalf, pp. 8-9.

and became important as foundation for the later reformers[37]. Among these early reformers was Shah Waliyullah Dahlavi. Historical accounts show us that his reforms were aimed at aspiring for the period of the Khulafa al-Rashidun. Shah Waliyullah wanted to create in India a stable Muslim rule reminiscent to the period of the "orthodox caliphate" in which the *'ulama* had an important role. He regarded the period in which there was no such Caliphate a period of regression because such a period failed to provide a balanced society. Shah Waliyullah is shown to have "understood the history to follow an evolutionary pattern in which the society evolved from the primitive orders to the universal orders. Even in its final evolutionary stage, it was thought that the institution of the Caliphate was necessary for a Caliph who would continuously enforce the shari'a and ensure an Islamic organization of society[38]. Muslims challenged the British control in 1857 when they joined the military uprising and the civil disorder it created. The British managed to suppress it. In the period of untold misery that came upon Muslims because of the brutal and ruthless suppression of the uprisings, the *'ulama* turned within, with one sole concern:

> "to preserve the religious heritage—the classic role of the *'ulama* from the post-Abbasid centuries on—and to disseminate instruction in authentic religious practice

---

[37] Among these reformers were Haj i Shariutullah (d. 1838), who had returned to India from the Wahabi dominated Hijaz and began defending Muslim interests against the British indigo planters and Hindu landlords. They insisted on fundamentals of Islam. Haji's s son, Dudhu Mian (d. 1862), also followed in his fathers footsteps and brought about greater religious consciousness particularly among the peasants.

[38] This is interesting because it further re-inforces in the mind of an Indian Muslim the necessity of a caliph, even when a society has progressed to reach its flowering in universal orders. We shall see Indian Muslims presenting similar arguments in the formation of the state of Pakistan.

and belief. They sought to be, and to create in others, personalities that embodied Islam. To this end, they preached and wrote, offered advisory legal opinions, and acted as spiritual guides to their followers"[39].

'These were the *'ulama* of the Deobandi movement and the Firangi Mahal. They strove for the preservation of the Caliphate. In this regard, and in direct support of the Khilafat movement, they formed in 1919, the *Jami'at al-'ulama al-Hind*. We shall see all these in the following chapters. On the basis of what has been described so far, it is not unreasonable to assume that in the mind of a common Indian Muslim, the authority of the universal caliph was accepted as a necessity. Since this was ingrained in their minds, it is not difficult to understand if Indian Muslims accepted wholeheartedly to go back to the practice of referring the caliph as the universal authority after the 1857 revolt, under the full support from their new rulers, the British empire. In the pages that follow, we shall see the full support the British government accorded Muslims to this notion; to the extent that the British government obtained a *fatwa* from the Ottoman sultan himself in this regard[40].

But first, we should look at the genesis of the institution of Caliphate, its influence upon Muslims in the initial years of the "orthodox caliphate" and the general history of its evolution, to the time when it was dismantled in 1924.

Although there are many *ahadith* reported to be traditions from the Prophet Muhammad in which he forecasts how the institution of the caliphate will function after him, the one that is most interesting is the one in which he prophesies its five

---

[39] Metcaff, pp. 11-12.

[40] Interestingly, sources show that even after the abolition of the Caliphate by the General National Assambly in 1924, Muslims in some part of India continued to name the Ottoman caliph in their Friday khutbas.

periods[41]. The fifth period will usher in the end of this world. The periods are:

1. his own period of *nubuwwa* (prophethood) in which he is the Caliph (vicegerent) of Allah on this earth, receiving direct communications from Him through the archangel Gabriel.

2. *khilafat minhaj al-nubuwa* in which the Caliphs after him are to follow the footsteps laid down by him[42].

3. the period of the *Mulkan 'Awdhan*, i.e. the era when the institution of the Caliphate is turned into dynasties. The rulers in this period, although referred to as the caliphs, are really autocratic rulers. The hadith implies they are to be cruel with little or no regard for basic human values. This period is interpreted as referring to the Umayyad, Abbasid, Seljuk and Ottoman dynasties.

---

[41]   see Abu Hajir Muhammad Said ibn Basyuni Zaghlul, *Musnad al-Imam Ahmed ibn Hanbal* (Beirut: Dar al-Kitab al 'Ilmiyya, 1989), vol. 4, p. 273. See also Maulana Abul Kalam Azad, *Khilafat and Jazirat al Arab* (Bombay: Central Khilafat Comitee, 1920).

[42]   This period lasted for 30 years after the demise of the prophet, ending with the Khulafa al-Rashidun. This period is believed to have ended when al-Hasan abdicated the Caliphate to Muawiyah of the Umayyads, who established for himself what is known in history as the Umayyad dynasty. The Shi`as have a different interpretation for this period. To them, this period does not refer to the Khulafa al-Rashidun. Rather, it refers to the Imams who Shi`as believe correctly guided the community, laying down for them the correct Shari'a, based on the Sunnah of the Prophet, for them to follow. This period would extend to 869 C.E. (255 A.H.), when the twelfth Shi`a Imam, Muhammad ibn al-Hasan al-Askari, is believed to have gone into occultation. It is this Imam who, it is believed, will return in the fifth period of the Prophet's prophecy to establish the caliphate of the Minhaj al-Nubuwwa. See n. 3. below.

4. the period of the Mulkan Jabriyyan, i.e., the period when Muslims are to be dominated, possibly colonized, by foreign powers. This has been interpreted as referring to the period that started with the discovery of the new world (late fifteenth century) by the Western powers until now.

5. the period of the *Khilafatan Minhaj al-Nubuwat*, i.e., the period that will see a return to following the footsteps laid down by the Prophet. This is the period Muslims say they are waiting for. In this period, as Muslims believe, the Mahdi (guide)[43] will be ushered in, accompanied by the return of 'Isa ibn Maryam (Jesus son of Mary)

Reflecting on the above hadith, which was being fully quoted by some Khilafat leaders[44] in India, one cannot help wondering what the Khilafat leadership was trying to achieve. Was the real purpose to use the Ottoman Caliphate as an instrument to achieve Indian Muslim objectives? In a pan-Islamic vision, Muslims in India could be recognized as a force that could not be neglected in any future participation in Indian politics. Theirs, it appears, was a desperate attempt to

---

[43] Shi`as believe this person will be their twelfth Imam who has been in occultation since 869 C.E. (255 A.H.). In this regard, they quote a hadi th from the Prophet: "*law lam yabqa min al-duniya illa yawmun wahidun latulu Allahu dhalika al-yam hatta yakhruju rajulun min ahli bayti yuwati'; ismuhu ismii wa kunniyatahu kuniyyatii yamlau al-ardhu 'adlan wa qistan kama mala'at jawran wa zulman*" (Even if there was only one day left to the life of this world, Allah will certainly extend that day until there appears a man from my household; his name will be my name (i.e. Muhammad! and whose genealogy will be my genealogy to fill the earth with justice and fairness just as it would have become filled with arrogance and oppression). See al-Fakhr al-Radi, Tafsir al-Kabir, vol. 1, p. 28.

[44] See for example Abul Kalam Azad, *Masala-i-Khilaf at wa Jazirat al-Arab* (Calcutta: Al-Balagh press, 1920), pp. 11ff.

coerce the British government into thinking that this institution had remained sacred and uninterrupted, without any blemishes over time, untarnished and infallible, and that its dismantling would provoke the wrath of Muslims everywhere. But the Ottoman empire, holder of the seat of the Caliphate at the time, was defeated in World War I. Britain, as the major power allied with France and Italy, was already preparing for the peace treaty to divide its territories. The interests of the British government lay more with the Arabs, who were themselves seeking to overthrow Ottoman control over them, than with the Ottoman empire. For a long time now, Britain had withdrawn its support of the Ottoman empire.

In Turkey itself, a movement was already launched to do away with the imperial past of the Ottoman Turks and secularize Turkey in order to bring it into line with the other modern nations of the time. The "Young Turks" were demanding a constitution[45]

---

[45] Young Turk movement led to the Young Turk Revolution of 1908. Its real beginnings were in 1860's when Sultan Abdul Aziz (1861-1876) tried to suppress any liberal ideas or reforms that were encouraged by his predecessor, Sultan Abdul Maj id (1839-1861). As Western liberal ideas were spreading in the Islamic world, the Turkish literary figures came into contact with Western literature. Their imagination was stirred by new culture and new ideas. New ideas aroused in them the feeling of Turkish nationalism. For the first time, they began to express it in their writings, with words like "parliament, constitution, and "fatherland". In 1864, the first liberal Young Turk journal called "*Hurriet* (Freedom), appeared in England. Soon the movement began to express political ideas. It began to demand adoption of a constitutional government in the Ottoman empire. Turks questioned the despotism and excesses of their Sultans. Under the reign of Abdul Hamid I1 (1876-1908), at least in the beginning, the programme for reforms was drafted. Abdul Hamid even promulgated, in 1876, a constitution for the Ottoman empire. For the first time in the history of the Ottoman empire a Parliament was convened in 1877, not to meet again

In India, in 1918, Muslims had become even more resentful and opposed to the British government as they blamed the collapse of Turkey squarely upon the shoulders of British government. More serious to Indians was the government's encroaching upon the Khilafat. Muslims were told by their leaders and had begun to think, as we shall see in ch. 2, that the government was going all out to destroy the last remaining symbol of Islam, the Caliphate. But at the beginning of the twentieth century, could the Caliphate in the hands of the Ottoman Turks, be considered a legitimate Islamic symbol Indian Muslims were wanting to preserve? The *hadith* of the Prophet quoted above and the historical evolution of the institution of the Caliphate would support the view that as an institution by itself, the caliphate had ceased to exist after al-Hasan abdicated it to Mu'awiya in 661 C.E?[46]

---

until the Young Turk Revolution of 1908. The Sultan had found an excuse with the war with Russia. Later, the Armenia massacres of the 1890's put a halt to his rising reputation in the West. The disenchanted Young Turks, under the influence of Western liberal ideas, revolted in the hope not to dismantle the Ottoman empire but to strengthen it by giving it a Western character. But this would lead later to the abolition of the institution of the Caliphate in 1924 when the Ottoman empire was defeated in the First World War. See Ernest Edmondson Ramsaur, *The Young Turks: Prelude to the Revolution of 1908* (Princeton: Princeton University Press, 19571, pp. 3-12. Also see M. Sukru Hanioglu, *The Young Turks in Opposition* (New York: Oxford University Press,1995).

[46] It can be argued, however, that the institution of the Caliphate itself ceased to exist immediately at the passing away of the Prophet in 632 C.E. In the argument that follows in this book, we shall see that in its exclusive sense, the Caliph is the one who receives direct communication from the Sovereign Lord. In this sense, we see Dawud (David) described in the Qur'an as the one who is told "We (God) have appointed you the Caliph . . .". The prophets are the recipients of the *wahy* (revelation), and therefore construed to be the sole Caliphs of God on the earth. Since Prophet Muhammad was the last in the chain of the prophets, he

This ended the period of the "rightly-guided" Caliphs, the *Khulafa al-Rashidun*, lasting 30 years after the passing away of the Prophet. The chronology of this institution from the time the Prophet passed away in 632 C.E. to the time when it was abolished by Turkey's newly elected Grand National Assembly in 1924 C.E. looks like this:

632-661 C.E. period of the *Khulafa al-Rashidun*

661-750 the Umayyad dynasty

750-1258 C.E. the Abbasids

(1261-1517 Abbasids in Cairo)

1261-1924 C.E. various monarchs throughout the Muslim world, particularly Ottoman Sultans, assuming the title of Caliphate indiscriminately. In the nineteenth century, with the advent of Western powers in the Near East, the Ottoman Sultan began to emphasize his role of a Caliph in order to gain support of Muslims living outside his realm. The Ottoman Empire collapsed in the First World War 1914-1918.

---

was the last direct Caliph of God on the earth. The institution of the Caliphate in this sense ended with him. I think his successors realised this, and it is for this reason they did not call themselves the Caliphs. Abu Bakr called himself the "Caliph of the Caliph" and his successor, Umar, initially called himself the "caliph of the Caliph of the Prophet of Allah". It was only because the title was getting to be a little awkward that it was shortened to the "Khalifa (Caliph) ". The notion that they were the actual Caliphs was something that developed later. In one Shi`a view, since the true Caliphs (successors) of the Prophet were the twelve Imams, their period ended only with the occultation of the Twelfth Imam in 869 C.E. (255 A.H.).

In March 1924, the Turkish Grand National Assembly abolished the Caliphate[47]. Kemal Ataturk is recorded to have said on 29th April 1910, "My friends and myself are going to stand up for the cause of old Islam to the last drop of blood".[48] Interestingly, by 1924 he was ready to abolish it with these words:

". . . the notion of a single Caliph exercising supreme religious authority over all the Muslim people, is one which has come out of books, not reality. The Caliph has never exercised over the Muslims a power similar to that held by the Pope over the Catholics . . . "[49]

With the end of the period of the four orthodox Caliphs in 661 C.E., Mu'awiya abandoned the main principle of this institution, namely, the process of election of the Caliph. Mu'awiya instituted instead a hereditary principle and clearly chose to establish a dynasty in the name of his clan, the Umayyads. The Umayyads ruled with racial pride and dominant aristocracy. It is important to note that Muslims in Makkah and Madina felt that instead of preserving the piety and simplicity of the Prophet and his companions, the Umayyad rule led by Mu'awiya had completely changed Caliphate making it more look like a temporal sovereignty "animated by worldly motives

---

[47] During the period 909-1171 C.B. another dynasty, the Fatimids, established themselves in North Africa and later in Egypt. They were Shi`a and they claimed infallibility. They were overthrown in 1171 by Salah al-Din - famous in the West under the name of Saladin.

[48] See Syed Mahmud, *The Khilafat and England*, (Patna: Mohemed Imtiyaz, 1921,)p. 9. See also "The Khilafat and England" in http://www.archive.org/stream/khilafatengland00mahm/ khilafatengland00mahm_djvu.txt.

[49] Hamid Enayat, *Modem Islamic Political Thought* (Austin: University of Texas Press, 1982), p. 54. See also "The Caliphate Question the Islamic Governance" in http://www.scribd.com/doc/80754308/.

and characterized by luxury and self-indulgence".[50] Mu'awiya was accused of having secularized the supreme power and exploiting the inheritance of the Muslim community for the benefit of his clan.

I think a situation was developing at this point that is anomalous compared with the ones established by the Prophet. The anomaly was that while Islam encouraged the combining of the state and religious affairs (Muhammad was the Prophet and a statesman at the same time), we find that after the period of the orthodox caliphate the legitimate theologians and jurists were increasingly devoting their energies in developing the corpus of shari 'a (religious law), whereas the matters of the state lay in the authority executed by the Umayyads. The Umayyads were building an empire. We see that by the time the Umayyad dynasty came to an end, it had created for itself a huge empire, stretching in the east from India to the borders of China, and westward from all territories of the Sasanian empire to the eastern provinces of the Roman empire and North Africa (but not Asia Minor). It also conquered Spain and sent troops across the Pyrenees.

The term "Caliph" received its prestige and grandeur from the greatness and riches it brought to this empire, although as already stated earlier, the title in its original meaning simply meant 'successor to the Messenger'. Umar was the first one to call himself also the *Amir al-Mu 'minin*[51]. Translated as 'the leader of believers', this title does not appear to be correct in light of the limited powers Umar carried as the Caliph. Sources tell us that the word amir has many meanings. It means 'king,' 'prince, 'lord,' 'governor,' 'leader of the blind,' 'a husband,' 'a counselor,' and 'advisor.'. In the context of the seat of the Caliphate at the time it only meant "counselor". This was

---

[50] Thomas W. Arnold, The Caliphate (Oxford: Clarendon Press, 1924), pp. 24-25.

[51] See Abi al-Hasan 'Ali bin al-Husayn al-Mas 'udi, *Ki tab bi Tanbih*, pp. 250-253.

conceived and understood both by Umar as well as Muslims. Umar was chosen a counselor with no powers to command since such powers were traditionally granted to the chief of the Arabian tribe.[52] This limitation on powers became hindrance to Umar as Islam was expanding rapidly to other lands. It is reported that he was contemplating restructuring the system when he died. Umar's successor was bound by the conditions of *shura*[53] to follow the practice of his predecessors and soon realized the annoyance of the limited powers. Uthman seems to have tried to assume more powers in his offices of *Amir al-Mu'minin*, at least in the autonomous provinces. Sources show that this was one cause of his murder[54]. As Islam spread to become a world empire, this title became very common. We are told[55] that in the Middle Ages, the Caliph was known in Europe by this title, sometimes spelt in many different ways, for example, "Elmiram Mommini", or "miralomin". The other title which also became widely used was "Imam"[56]. The Imam,

---

[52] See M.A. Shaban, *The Abbasid Revolution* (Cambridge: University Press, 1970), pp. 140-141.

[53] When Umar was dying, he appointed a shura (consultative committee) of six possible successors to elect from among them one who would succeed him. 'Ali seemed to all members to be the right choice; but 'Ali rejected the condition that apart from the Qur'an and the Sunnah he would also follow the decisions laid by his predecessors. Ali rejected this condition. Uthman accepted and became the next Caliph after Umar.

[54] Shaban, pp. l4lff.

[55] Arnold, p. 33

[56] The more modern scholarship tells us that the notion Imam as the leader of the Muslim community is a Shi`a definition. An Imam in the Shi`a tradition is one who possesses special attributes that are endowed upon him from the realm of knowledge, *'ilm al-Ladduni*. Through intuition (but not revelation), an Imam receives divine guidance through which many problems of the Muslim community are solved. Abu Bakr certainly did not claim any such powers. The title Abu Bakr maintained was *Khalifat Rasul Allah*, with no powers of the Prophet. The Shi`a sects wanted an Imam to occupy the

in the sense applied in Sunni Islam, simply meant the leader of prayers. One of the functions of the *Amir al-Mu'minin* was to lead the five daily prayers. In this sense, the Caliph was also the "Imam"[57]. Although the three titles (Caliph, *Amir al-Mu'minin* and Imam) described the same person, the title that stands out describing him as a successor to the Prophet was "Caliph". The title combined in it all the three meanings and recognized him also as a temporal leader of the Islamic state. In the Qur'an, the term "Caliph" (Khalifa) is used both in general as well as specific terms. In general tems, the verse quoted most when describing the institution of Caliphate in modern times is in chapter 24, 'The Light', Verse 55. This verse reads :

"Allah hath promised unto those of you who believe and do good deeds that He will certainly appoint them successors in the earth *(layastakhlifannahum fi al-ardhi)* as He appointed successors before them, and that certainly He shall establish for them their religion (Islam) which He hath chosen for them, and that certainly He will, after their fear, in exchange give them security; they shall worship Me; and associating not with Me aught; and whosoever disbelieveth after this, these! they are the wicked ones."

In specific tems, the Qur'an refers in ch. 38:26 to Dawud (David)[58] : "0 Dawud! verily We have appointed thee a khalifa (Caliph) in the earth". And in ch. 2 :30 referring to Adam: "Verily, I intend to appoint a (Caliph) in the earth." Similarly,

---

office of *Amir al-Mu'minin* with both the secular as well as religious powers.

[57] The title first appeared on coins during the Abbasid reign of Mamun (813-833). Abbasid caliphs took on a more religious character in their positions as caliphs. They encouraged religious discussions in their courts. They passionately upheld and enthusiastically participated in religious discussions.

[58] In Islam, Dawud (David) is considered to be among the *anbiya* (prophets).

we find several traditions from the Prophet recorded in several books relating to the caliphs. In a very interesting exchange that took place between Abu Bakr and one of the *Ansar* (helpers) at the time of Abu Bakr's election was the issue of who, among the *Ansar* (helpers who gave refuge to Muslims in Medina after their migration, the *hijrah*), had more right to be a caliph. Abu Bakr reminded the *Ansar* that the candidate had to be from the *umara'* (that is, the rulers, in this case the Qurayshites) ; whereas the *Ansar* would be the *wuzara'* (that is, the deputies)[59]

So why, then, was the twentieth-century Khilafat movement in India launched to support an institution that was at the time by no means neither from the *umara* nor fitting in the pattern of *minhaj al-Nabuwwa*? Perhaps this lack was realised by the Abbasids as well as the Ottomans. For this reason, both the Abbasids and the Ottomans tried to raise their status by using for themselves other honorific titles. For example, Abbasids used titles like "shadow of God on earth". A rebel who was once brought before the Abbasid caliph al-Mutawakkil in 849 C.E. addressed him "as the rope stretched out between God and His creatures". Al-Mansur, the second Abbasid caliph, declared in 775C.E. that he was the "sultan of God upon His earth." Perhaps one reason that they claimed to be why the Abbasids became acceptable was the descendants of 'Abbas, the uncle of the Prophet. They gained support for their revolution against the Umayyads because they claimed to be the Shi'a of Ali. In

---

[59] In an interesting speech Abu Bakr gave, he said to the Ansar, "We are the first people in Islam; and among the Muslims, our abode is the centre, our descent is noblest, and we are nearer to the Prophet in relation; and you (Ansar) are our brothers in Islam and our partners in religion; you helped us, protected us and supported us, may Allah reward you His best. So we are the rulers *(umara')* and you are the deputies *(wuzara')* . . . therefore do not compete with your brothers in what Allah has bestowed upon them." See S.H.M. Jafri, The Origins and Early Development of Shi 'a Islam (London: Longman, 1979), p. 46.

this they mustered huge support from Shi`as who were already very disappointed with the Umayyads because of Mu'awiya's and his successors' attitude towards `Ali and the Ahl al-Bayt (people of the household of the Prophet) generally. Support also came from other disgruntled minorities who had openly revolted against what they felt were the unjustified practices of the Umayyads. These were the major reasons of the Umayyad declines[60] Sources tell us that the practice of *Jahiliyya* (the era of pre-Islamic paganism) had come back to flourish in the time of the Umayyads. The Urnayyad rulers showed favors to the members of their own clan.

The Abbasids reached their zenith in the year 800 C.E. This date has a parallel with Charlemagne in Rome and the establishment of the Holy Roman Empire. After 800 C.E., the authority of the Abbasid caliphate began to decline. There are several reasons for this to have happened. First, in the same year, the Aghlabids set up their own dynasty in North Africa. A separate dynasty also arose in Persia. Gradually, Egypt and Syria also separated themselves. By the tenth century, Abbasid authority hardly extended beyond Baghdad. The `Abbasid Khulafa were at the mercy of foreign troops.

Some Abbasid Caliphs became unpopular also because of their drunkenness, sensuality and extravagance. One such example was the Abbasid caliph, al-Muqtadir (908-932), who was deposed twice. Almost all his successors were the puppets of Turkish troops in the army. They were either deposed, jailed and blinded or had to flee to take refuge with friendly dynasties in the region. Another Abbasid caliph, al-Mustakfi, had to welcome the Buwayhids as a controlling element in Baghdad in 945. The Buwayhids were Shi`as, and Abbasids who were

---

[60]   During the revolution an Umayyad prince fled and established himself in 756 in Spain. In 928, Abd al-Rahman 111, an Umayyad ruler in Spain, ordered he should be styled as Khalifa and Amir al-Mu'minin.

Sunnis were under their control. Their authority remained paramount, and they exerted it for at least a century.

Since Buwayhids were Shi`as, they did not really recognize the claim that a Sunni caliph had the ultimate authority in Islam. Their names were read in the *khutba* (Friday sermons) along with the name of the caliph. In the Buwayhid period, the Abbasid Caliphate reached its lowest point. The Caliph's use of his title was only ceremonial, particularly if it was in the interest of the Buwayhids.

It is interesting that a Qurayshite Amir of Makkah decided to take advantage of the declining authority of the Abbasid caliphate. He promoted himself among the population for his right to be a caliph since he was an Arab and a Qurayshite. He tried to seek alliance with the Banu Tayy tribe but changed his mind, and returned to Makkah as fast as he had left it.

With the situation at the lowest point[61] for the Caliphate as an institution, it was only the theory of one of the most

---

[61] The institution of the Caliphate had reached the point of total degradation. First, North Africa became independent as Aghlabids established their own dynasty. Other provinces were to follow this including Persia. At the time of the Abbasid revolution, an Umayyad prince had managed to escape and established himself in Andalusia (Spain). Egypt and Syria were cut off. By the tenth century, the Abbasid caliph's authority was limited only to Baghdad and that too was totally at the mercy of undisciplined foreign troops mainly from Turkey. In 928, 'Abd al-Rahman in Andalusia proclaimed himself the Caliph after the Abbasid Caliphs al-Muqtadir and Qahir were blinded because of the internal feud. The succeeding Caliphs were under the mercy of Turkish generals. Qahir was thrown into prison for eleven years. Another Caliph, al-Muttaqi, had to flee to Mosul under the protection of Hamdanid princes. In Baghdad, the Turkish general Tuzun set up the puppet caliph al-Mustaqfi. When Tuzun died, al-Mustaqfi invited the Shi`a Buwayhids.

distinguished jurists, Abu al-hasan 'Ali ibn Muhammad ibn Habib al-Basri al-Baghdadi al-Mawardi (ca. 1058), that seems to have rescued the institution of the Caliphate from total collapse[62].

I think Mawardi's theory[63] was an important consideration in the minds of the Khilafat leaders in India. The Khilafat leaders, it would seem, used Mawardi's theory as their intellectual resource upon which they could base their arguments. Mawardi was also the *qadi* (judge in the Shari'a court) and a *mufassir* (commentator) of the Qur'an. Mawardi theorised that the institution of the Caliphate was valid and must be supported. According to him, a candidate had to meet the criteria qualified by the Islamic Shari'a. The criteria to be met by a candidate were that: the Caliph must be a male of an upright lifestyle, of good character, mature in age (an adult in Islamic Shari'a, at least 15 years old), and a Qurayshite. Mawardi said that the history of this institution had thus far shown that it remained elective, and although it was not strictly in the hands of the Quraysh, Mawardi maintained, a caliph had always nominated a successor. He said it was not clear in Sunni *fiqh* (jurisprudence) how many electors had to be present before the election was valid or even how many representatives would have to be present on behalf of the whole community. Mawardi pointed out

---

[62] al-Hasan 'Ali ibn Muhammad ibn Habib al-Basri al-Baghdadi al-Mawardi was a native of Basra and one of the most distinguished and eminent jurisconsults of the Shafi'i sect. Mawardi composed many works dealing with theology and sociology of Islam. His work relating to the Caliphate is *al-Ahkam al-Sultaniyyah* (The Laws of Islamic Governance), Tr. by Asadullah Yate (London, 1996).

[63] AL-Mawardi listed ten functions in his book, *al-Ahkam i-Sultaniyah*. These included not only the enforcement of law and defence and expansion of the realm of Islam but included also a law that a Caliph had a duty to enforce the Shari'a and also defend Islam and expand it. This made the Caliphst role spiritual as well as temporal. See Glenn E. Perry, "Caliphs" in Encyclopedia of Islam, pp.239-40.

it could be witnessed even by just two persons or any number of persons. He reached a conclusion that a Caliph can appoint his own successor and yet it would be considered as though he was elected[64].

Another scholar, al-Biruni (d. 1075), realising the state of degradation the Caliphate had reached, said that what was left of the institution was merely dogmatic rituals. He said the Caliphate had become a lame-duck and had not much authority left where it could exercise and had become only a ceremonial figure. There are many examples where it is seen that an Abbasid caliph had been disabled by the Buwayhids from exercising any authority and the caliph had become only a ceremonial figure. An example of this is given in one of the incidents in the time of a Buwayhid prince 'Adud al-Dawla (the Hand-or Strength-of the State). This Buwayhid prince, in order to glorify his own position, made the Abbasid caliph to confer upon him the title of sultan by crowning him with a jewelled crown and bestowing upon him other royal insignia. All this was done in elaborate ceremonies. 'Adad al-Dawla also made the Caliph consent to the insertion of al-Dawlah's name in the Friday sermons. This, we are told, was the "lowest depths of degradation that the Caliphate . . . had ever reached[65].

On another occasion, a prince of Fatimid Egypt was visiting Baghdad. In an elaborate ceremony prepared by 'Adud al-Dawla, the Caliph was made to sit on a high throne with the mantle of the Prophet hung on his shoulders and the copy of the Qur'an placed before him. 'Adud al-Dawlah entered this majestic arrangement and kissed the ground before the Caliph seven times as he proceeded forward to kiss the hands of the Caliph with a show of the utmost reverence and respect. This kind of ceremony, if created to impress envoys of other places, certainly worked, as the envoys left Baghdad feeling awe-struck at the majesty of the Abbasid caliphs and the reverence and

---

[64] See Mawardi, pp. 5-7. See also Arnold, pp.70 if.

[65] Arnold, p.65.

respect they received from their subjects. In actual fact, it was a period of horror for most of the Abbasid caliphs.

Nizami Arudi, yet another scholar of the twelfth century, agrees with Mawardi, but he also extends the theory to include rulers of all other dynasties who had proclaimed themselves caliphs in their own provinces. Arudi says that it was absolutely necessary in Islam to maintain the Shari'a law. In the absence of the Prophet this was done by his caliph(successor) who is really the Imam. But since the Imam cannot physically be present in a vast Islamic empire at one and the same time, there is a need to have his representatives who are really the *na`ibain,* or the representatives of the Caliph in Baghdad.

Ibn Khaldun (1332-1406) theorised that since the fundamental base of any empire is the religion, men must be guided by the Rasul Allah (the messenger of God) or one who takes his place, i.e. the Caliph. It is the caliph that guides man in the principle of Shari'a, and therefore, his (caliph's) validity cannot be denied. Ibn Khaldun rejected philosophers who said a caliph is only necessary because it is only rational to have a leader for an orderly society. Ibn Khaldun argued by saying that it was not only rational but theologically it was essential. Ibn Khaldun argued in favour of the caliphate but at the same time agreed that the Umayyads had turned despots and agreed further that the essential features of the caliphate had disappeared.

It was because of theories like this, and particularly Mawardi's theory at the time when the caliphate was going through the period of degradation, that it was re-inforced in its theological importance. The Indian Khilafat leaders played heavily on this issue, emphasising the theological need for the institution of the caliphate[66]

---

[66] The Indian Khilafat leaders were not entirely wrong in their historical context. We have seen that throughout the period of the institution of the Abbasid caliphate, the caliph remained for

We are shown in sources an interesting parallel in the history of the Holy Roman Empire in the time when the emperor Frederick III was driven out of Vienna during the fifteenth century. While he was virtually reduced to the level of a beggar and the only money he could make was by conferring titles, his contemporary jurist, in fact Pope Pius II, decreed that the power of the emperor was eternal and could not be reduced or injured in any way. Non-believers of this were branded by Pope Pius II as heretics since he had ordained this "by Holy Writ and by the decree of the Church"[67]

The Caliph was still therefore, at least in theory, a head of an Islamic state, and even though powerless in the face of military control, he still was fully honoured and respected in public, and as we have seen even by the Buwayhids.

What weakened the Buwayhids was the rise of another power in the sphere of Persian influence, the Seljuks. These were a Turkish people, who eventually overtook the Buwayhids completely under the leadership of Tughril in the year 1055.[68]

---

the majority of Sunni Muslims a successor of the Prophet. He was to be honoured, and in madressas throughout the Islamic world Muslim children were taught that the Caliph was the *Amir al-Mu 'minin* (leader of the faithful). What the Khilafat leaders at the time failed to realise, I. think, was that the institution of the Caliphate had also gone through a social evolution. The time for a one-man caliph had evolved and the necessity was for a collective body of Muslims to function in the role of a caliph. This would come through *ijtihad* and as we shall see. in the succeeding chapters, this is exactly what seems to have happened, but only after the abolition of the caliphate by the National Assembly of Turkey and the collapse of the Khilafat movement in India.

[67]   See Arnold, P. 78.

[68]   With the caliphate and the conquest of Baghdad in 1055 by the Seljuks, a new distinction between the caliphate and the sulatanate emerged. The office of the sultanate came to be held by the effective ruler, the Seljuk Sultan. The office of the caliphate itself

The 'Abbasids were so much suppressed by the Buwayhids that they wholeheartedly supported the campaigns of the Seljuks and proclaimed them to be the "deliverers". The Caliph conferred upon him the title "Sultan of the East and west."[69].

But soon they, too, began to oppress the Abbasid caliphs. At least one caliph, al-Mustarshid (1118-1134), attempted to raise an army to overthrow the Seljuk overlord, but in the process, got himself killed.

Still, the institution of the Caliphate enhanced the prestige of the 'Abbasids. However, what was still in store for this dynasty was the horror of 1258 C.E. The Mongol invasion of Baghdad was cruel enough, but when the Mongol army, under Hulagu, put the Caliph of the time, al-Mu'tasim, to death, people were stunned. That a Caliph could be put to death in the manner Mu'tasim was, was a matter of incredible bewilderment for many Muslims who saw in the office of the Caliphate a continuity of divine guidance[70].

Interestingly, Mawardi's theory of the caliphate seems to have solidified the institution to the extent that it created around it an aura of its own. Thus, Hulagu, the Mongol leader who invaded Baghdad in 1258, was warned by Muslims accompanying his army that if he shed the blood of the Caliph al-Mu'tasim, the whole "world would be overspread with darkness and the army of the Mongols would be swallowed up by the earthquake."[71]

---

came to be restricted mainly to the role of a ceremonial monarch who would legitimise the rule to those who held real power, See *EI*, p. 240

[69] See Arnold, p. 80.

[70] Al-Mu'tasim was put into a sack and tied behind horses to be dragged alive to his death. Baghdad was stunned at this.

[71] See Arnold, p. 81.

It was only after the Mongols consulted a great jurist and philosopher, Shaykh Nasir al-Din al-Tusi (ca. 1274), to predict whether divine vengeance would follow, that Hulagu felt confident to carry on with his plans.

Muslims had on the whole become used to the idea of the Caliphate. They found it totally incredible that for the very first time since the passing away of the Prophet the Muslim body was without a caliph. The bewilderment and the vacuum felt is seen in the lamenting verse Muslims recite when facing extreme difficulty.[72]

This was an incredible and unprecedented event. Their bewilderment and suffering is seen in the following supplication which was offered in the Grand Mosque in Baghdad on a Friday following the destruction the Abbasid Caliphate and the destruction of the beautiful capital city itself.

> "Praise be to Allah who has caused exalted personages to perish and has given over to destruction the inhabitants of this city . . . 0 Allah, help us in our misery, the like of which Islam and its children have never witnessed; we are Allah's and unto Allah do we return."[73]

The vacuum created by the absence of a Caliph was acutely felt, especially by the leaders of breakaway regimes. Although they had broken away from the Abbasid rule, their authority and prestige depended really upon their being accepted and invested with titles by the caliph in Baghdad. Such regimes

---

[72] See Qur'an 2:155-156, "Be sure We shall test you with something of fear and hunger, some loss in goods or lives or fruits (of your toil), but give glad tidings to those who persevere, who say when afflicted with calamity: *"Innalillahi wa inna Ilayhi raji'un"* (Verily we are Allah's and unto Allah do we return).

[73] 'Quoted in Arnold (p. 82) from C. d'Ohsson, *Histoire des Mongols*, vol. iii, pp. 251-254.

stretched from northern India westward to North Africa. The Mamluk dynasty in Egypt felt an acute need for an investiture from a caliph if they were to enjoy any authority in their territories. Luckily for them, at the onslaught on Baghdad by the Mongols in 1258, one of the Abbasid princes managed to escape. The Mamluks invited him with great pomp and ceremony to install him as the caliph. He assumed the title al-Mustansir in June 1261 and conferred upon the Mamluk Sultan Baybars great honour and a diploma of investiture. Thus Mamluks became fully established in Cairo and gained immense prestige for having re-instituted the Caliphate.

Mamluks were actually Turkish slaves and had taken over from the decaying Ayyubid dynasty which was originally founded by Salah al-Din. It is interesting that upon al-Mustansir becoming an Abbasid Caliph in Cairo, this new lease upon the Abbasids also meant that he became the Caliph of those lands which had previously been never under the Abbasids while they were in Baghdad. The 'Abbasids remained in Cairo for almost 250 years after that.

The institution of the Caliphate endured also because of Muslim philosophers who in their treatises clearly showed the need of a Caliph for a harmonious society. Thus, a great Islamic philosopher, al-Farabi (870-950), who witnessed the weakening powers of the Abbasid caliphs, had worked out a theory of an ideal state. In this theory, which was obviously influenced by Platonic doctrine, al-Farabi showed that the goal of a man is to be guided so that his soul could understand the source (i.e., the first existence in Platonic theory) from which it emanated and would long to return to that source. Al-Farabi pointed out that just as the universe is a cosmos wholly under the supreme authority of God, and contains graded existences which are all orderly and harmonious, so is the human spirit made up of successive degrees of intelligence. The human body is an organized whole over which presides his heart. So is the state an organism or graded system which can remain in harmony only when it is under the guidance of a philosopher leader who rules with love and justice. With some Muslims, this theory came to be applied to the theory of the Caliphate.

Other philosophers included the *Ikhwan al-Safa*, who dealt with every branch of philosophy and clearly laid down the doctrine of the caliphate. They said that the kings really are the caliphs because they are the vicegerents of God on this earth. It is only He who gave them the authority to rule on His earth, over His creatures with justice and equity.

Another philosopher, Shihab al-Din Suhrawardi (1153-1191), died young because he was put to death for heresy. He produced a philosophy of illumination in which he proclaimed that the world has never been without philosophy, the manifest proof of which is the caliph. This will endure for as long as the heaven and earth endures.

These theories and others like them, where a caliph is seen as an epitome of virtue and justice, were popularized. In some instances the Seljuks tried to put these theories into practical use in the administration of their judicial military and other branches. In the later part of the eleventh century one of the popular notions was that "in every age God selects a man whom He adorns with kingly qualities and to whom he entrusts the well-being and the peace of His servants."[74]

A philosopher and jurist who had no sympathy for the institution of the Caliphate was Shaykh Nasir al-Din al-Tusi (d. 1274). As mentioned above, he did not agree with the general belief, at the time when Baghdad was sacked by Hulagu, that destruction of the Caliph would bring about divine vengeance. He advised Hulagu to proceed with his plans. Shaykh al-Tusi was a Shi`a, and his just and ideal ruler was the Imam. He produced a philosophical work which was later adopted by Jalal al-Din Dawani in 1470 and was dedicated to the Ottoman rulers. In this works he uses theological arguments to show

---

[74]   Arnold (p. 125) quoting from *Siyasat-Nameh*.

that a Caliph has a duty to uphold the Shari'a, which makes him not only the Caliph with all the titles that go with that, but also a lieutenant of the Prophet. Perhaps the most important contribution he made to validate the institution of the Caliphate for all non-Arab rulers was that in his theory he made use of the Qur'anic verses to show that a caliph need not necessarily be from the Quraysh. It was as if the caliph derived his authority directly from God.

Thus, when the Ottomans rose to power, they regarded themselves as the ones who were endowed with the dignity of a caliph. We find therefore that when Murad I conquered Adrianople and Philippopolis in 362, he was congratulated by the Amir of Karamania in a letter describing him with titles like "the chosen Khalifa of the Creator". It is interesting to read Murad's reply. He wrote that while there was no difference among the rulers and their subjects, God has bestowed upon some of His chosen ones the dignity of the Caliphate so that they are more responsible in that they relieve the misery of the poor and the helpless. Other dignitaries addressed Murad I with titles like "Your highness who (is) Sultan of the Sultans of Islam, and *Khaqan* of the *Khaqans* of mankind".

The Ottoman emperor to have the highest title was Muhammad the II, who established the capital of the Turkish empire at Constantinople. The titles he received surpassed all the other titles. He was called "his majesty who has attained to the preeminent rank of the Khilafat, the refuge of the Sultanate". One letter ends with a prayer, "May Allah Almighty multiply the days of his Sultanate and increase the years of his life and his Khilafat (caliphate) until the day of Judgement"[75].

The Ottomans went on to crush Persian forces at Chaldiran in 1514, thus putting an effective check to the growing influence of Shah Isma'il. The Ottoman Sultan to succeed in doing this was Salim, who then went on to check the great

---

[75]   Arnold, p. 134.

power of the Mamluk regime, seat of the Abbasid caliph, as we have already seen. The Mamluks, too, were defeated in 1516.

There is no clear account to show what happened to the Caliph al-Mutawakkil. In some sources we are told Salirn sent him to Constantinople for a while and when he found out that the Caliph was involved in buying dancing girls for his amusement, Salim imprisoned him. After Salim died, al-Mutawakkil was released and sent to Cairo as a puppet caliph.

In another report, it appears that after the conquest of Egypt, al-Mutawakkil transferred his caliphate to Salim. The transfer included all the relics a caliph is required to have, such as the mantle believed to be from the time of the Prophet, the copy of the Qur'an believed to be from the time of Uthman and the sword believed to be of 'Ali ibn Abi Talib[76]

Salim achieved greatness and power no other caliph had ever enjoyed because of his total control over most of the civilized world of the time. He also became the guardian of Makkah and Madina. To any ruler, this was the highest symbol of prestige. As we shall see in succeeding chapters, the Khilafat Movement Committee in India accused the Sharif of Makkah of coveting the position where he could become the guardian of the two most sacred sanctuaries of Islam.

---

[76] It was this transfer that appears to have enabled the subsequent Ottoman sultans to make an official claim to be the caliphs. The first appearance of this is in the eighteenth century when in the Treaty of Kuchuk Kaynarja was signed in 1774 between Russia and the Ottoman empire. The Ottoman Sultan was officialy recognised as a caliph of Islam. It is likely true, as the sources tell us, that there was a confusion i n the minds of Western leaders who viewed the Ottoman sultanate as the Islamic counterpart of the papacy and of the Russian ruler's role as head of the Orthodox Church. See *EI*, pp. 239-240.

We have already seen earlier that with their rise, the Ottomans came to believe that their authority was divinely appointed. The direct result of this was the avoidance of the title of caliphate or caliph in the official documents. Also, the Ottomans adopted the Hanafi school of legal thought in Islam. The Hanafi school held that the true caliphate ended with the *Khulafa al-Rashidun* (the first four caliphs). This became the accepted view, and hence the title Sultan became preferred. However, in some forms of address, the Sultan was referred to as either "Khilafat martabat" or "Rauzat al Khilafatu" or "janab-i-Khilafat" [77].

This, however, began to change beginning in the eighteenth century, when foreign powers began to make inroads into the rich Islamic world. One of the very first signs of this was in the treaty signed with Russia in 1774. In the Treaty of Kuchuk Kaynarja between Sultan 'Abdul Hamid and the Empress of Russia, the Sultan recognised independence for its Tartaric population of the Crimea and Kuban in northern Russia. These regions were inhabited also by a Christian population belonging to the Orthodox Church. The Empress had claimed to be their patroness and Muslims claimed a similar relationship to the Ottoman Sultan. Thus in the treaty, Sultan Abdul Hamid is referred to as the caliph. This preserved the Shari'a law for Muslims with the Sultan as the chief caliph of the Islamic Shari'a[78].

---

[77] The words "janab", "rauzat" and "Martabat" are used when addressing highly respected dignitaries or highly regarded elderly members in a family or in a community. These forms simply express reverence and respect. Here all the three forms carry the meaning equivalent to the Latin "your highness." More specifically, they refer to "the one who represents the Caliphate of the dignified *Khulafa al-Rashidun.*

[78] With the Treaty of Kuchuk Kaynarja signed in 1774, the Ottoman Sultan was officially recognised as the Caliph of Islam. This was likely to happen some day, even for political reasons, because the Ottoman Sultans were already the holders of the Mantle of

Interestingly, then, in the sixteenth century, the Hanafi school refused to recognize an Ottoman Sultan as the caliph because, as we have already seen earlier, they believed that the true caliphate ended with the *Khulafa al-Rashidun*. Yet in the eighteenth century, it appears all doctrines were put aside because it became politically necessary to do so. One reason for this could also be that when the rule of Islamic law is threatened, one could use reason to maintain the continuity of the rule of Islamic law. In such situations, the fundamental requirement would be that nothing should be done to violate the basic principles of Islam such as, worship of One God, the Five Pillars of Islam and social justice for all. It seems the Khilafat Committee in India were well aware of this and were prepared to go to considerable lengths to see that the Ottoman caliphate was maintained. Interestingly, this view was also endorsed by the Hanafi jurisprudent because they said it had become necessary to maintain Islamic unity in the face of Western domination. However, it did not take too long for the Western powers to become a dominating force. World War I in the beginning of the twentieth century brought about the defeat of the Ottoman empire and the Ottoman Caliphate itself was being threatened[79].

For Muslims in India this was a great blow for several reasons, as we shall see in the following chapters. Muslims had been a dominating power in India from the Mughal times. Indeed, during the sixteenth and the seventeenth centuries, as far as the seat of the caliphate was concerned, the only rival the Ottomans had was the Mughal empire[80]. The Mughal

---

the Prophet and other relics transferrred to them by the defeated Abbasid Caliph al Mutawakkil in 1512.

[79] The Ottoman empire was defeated against Britain. The Ottomans had decided to side with Germany in World War I.

[80] Interestingly, from the early sixteenth century to the end of eighteenth, almost the whole of the huge Islamic territory was under the hands of the three great empires. These were the Ottoman, the Mughal and the Safavids. Although they shared

emperors not only assumed the title of caliph but also during the reign of Akbar they called their capital *Dar al-Khilafat* (the abode of the Caliphate). Their coins bore an inscription which read "the great Sultan, the exalted caliph". The only advantage the Ottoman Sultans possessed to rank them greater than the Mughal emperors lay in the fact that they were also the protectors of the two sanctuaries, Makkah and Madina.

Thus in 1919, the Khilafat leaders realized that in supporting Britain and the Allied forces[81], Muslims had actually helped weaken the only seat of the Islamic symbol of Islamic rule. Indian Muslim leaders came to fear that with Hindu demands for concessions from the British they might be reduced to insignificance even in India. In this context, the Khilafat Movement became for them a worthy cause. Not

---

the common Turco-Mongol heritage and had a similar style in administration of their respective territories, they were preoccupied with their own internal problems. See Aziz Ahmad, *Studies in Islamic Culture in the Indian Environment* (Oxford : Clarendon Press, 1964), p. 22. As far as the seat of the caliphate was concerned, the Safavids, who had established themselves in Iran from 1502, were no threat to the Mughals or to the Ottomans. The Safavids were Shi`as and had established themselves basing their claims on the theology of Imamate rather than Caliphate.

[81] There are several tracts in the Proscribed Material criticising Muslims for having sided with the British government and its allied forces. See for example, essays by Sayyid Sulaiman Ashraf, *al-Balagh: Musalmanon ke tanazzul ke asbab aur Khilafa t-Usmaniyyah ke tarikhi Vaqiat*. See also in the same tract, Aligarh: Muhammad Faruq, entry number 1579. Two esssays examine the decline of Muslim states, especially Ottoman Turkey. The first essay blames it on Muslims abandonment of the path of Islam and the European hostility towards them. The second essay examines the Islamic policies in regard to politics, war and Khilafat. The essays urge Muslims not to abandon the path of Islam, but to return to its basics, that is, the Qur'an and the*Sunna*.

all Khilafat leaders thought along this lines, of course. There were leaders in the Khilafat committee who sincerely believed that their cause would redeem them from the sin they had committed to ally themselves with Britain and the Allied forces; and some others believed that Britain, as true power for the Muslims in the world, would never infringe upon the caliphate, but on the contrary would promote it. For yet others, it was a true cause for Islam. And then there were others like Muhammad Ali Jinnah and Muhammad Iqbal, who while supporting what the Khilafat movement stood for, vehemently opposed the style of the Khilafatist leaders. Their views were to emerge later in the Pakistan movement.

In any case, it was felt that the restoration of the Caliphate was necessary. Besides the historical claims for legitimacy sketched so far, there were several other factors giving importance to this cause in the minds of Indian intellectuals. It is to these that we now turn.

CHAPTER TWO:

THE RE-EMERGENCE OF THE IDEA OF THE CALIPHATE IN THE MINDS OF INDIAN MUSLIMS

Almost at the threshold of the twentieth century, Muslims in India were finding their political consciousness considerably aroused. There were several reasons for this to happen.

First, there was a shift in the British government's policy towards the Ottoman empire. This shift began about 1877 when the British government decided it was in its best interest not to aid the Ottoman empire in Russo-Turkish wars. We are told that

". . . the disillusionment of the consensus of Indo-Muslim intelligentsia began in 1877-8 over the lack of effective British aid to the Turks against the Russians, the policy of the British Liberal party, and the political intrigues . . ."[82].

Prior to this time, Muslims in India had been satisfied that their Christian rulers were getting on well with the only major Muslim power of the time[83]

---

[82] Aziz Ahmad, "Sayyid Ahmad Khan Jamal al-Din al-Afghani and Muslim India", Studica Islamica 13 (1960)pp.68-69

[83] After the 1857 uprisings against the British rule in India, the only other Muslim power Indian Muslims recognised was the Mughal empire. Symbolically, this existed until 1857. After the uprisings that year, the British government in crushing the uprisings, shot and killed the nobles of the Mughal empire. The Mughal emperor himself, Bahadur Shah Zafar, was sent in exile to Burma where he eventually died. The Mughal empire was thus totally annihilated.

Second, this shift in the British government's policy towards the Ottoman empire forced upon Muslims in India a choice between loyalty to the British government and sympathy for *Dar al-Islam* (abode of Islam)[84]." Muslims were clearly beginning to opt for *Dar al-Islam* because in the shift of policy Indian Muslims felt the British government was engaging itself in a conspiracy to destroy Islamic civilisation and its values. Muslims based their belief upon the events they saw unfolding both outside India as well as in India in which they felt the British government to be supporting the European powers in their systematic military campaigns against the Ottoman empire.

Outside of India, they first saw in 1859 the Franco-Spanish aggression against Morocco. This led to the Algeciras Act in 1906, in which Morocco was forced to sign a treaty providing trading facilities to England, France, Germany and Spain[85]. 'Then there were the Russo-Turkish wars, in which Muslims saw the British government not only withdrawing its support of

---

Thereafter, the Ottoman empire remained for Muslims in India, the only Muslim power.

[84]   Aziz Ahmad, "Sayyid Ahmad Khan," p. 69.

[85]   The troubles really began when Abdul Rahrnan of the Hussainian dynasty died. Spain and France, as the leading powers in the area, intervened to force the enthronement of Sidi Muhammad. The Moroccan army objected to a foreign power's interfering and raided Spanish and Franco-Algerian territory. Spain and France saw the opportunity and used this as a pretext to declare war against Morocco. The Franco-Spanish army won the war and forced upon Morocco the Peace of Tetuan treaty in 1860. Part of Morocco's territory was annexed, and Christian missionaries were allowed to propagate Christianity through out Morocco. Much to the horror of Muslims in India, the British consented to France, annexing the whole territory. It was only at the intervention of Germany that Algeciras Act was signed, superseding any earlier treaty. See Shan Muhammad, Freedom Movement in India: The Role of Ali Brothers, (New Delhi, Associated Publishing House, 1939), p. 18.

the Ottoman empire but also aligning itself with the European powers. Thus in the 1878 Congress of Berlin the British government managed to enhance its power and hold over the Middle East.'

The Balkan states were anxiously watching these developments very carefully. When it became apparent to them that the Ottoman empire was heavily engaged defending itself from attack by European nations, they took the opportunity to attack the Ottoman empire themselves. They were convinced that they, too, would be successful if they launched a concerted attack. The Balkan states revolted with the full support from people of neighboring Bulgaria and also of thousands of volunteers who enrolled themselves under the Serbian flag. We are told that

> All these things working together produced a remarkable effect[86]. The progress of the unfortunate events in Balkan states were anxiously watched by Mussalrnans of India . . . (they saw that) . . . the British government could not help Turkey against its enemies for the dream of the dismemberment of the dominions of Sick man of Europe.

The Balkan states campaigned against the Ottoman Turks, propagating to show them as an uncivilized and tyrant nation. That this was only a political game was confirmed later when a Serbian General Mijatovich, representing Serbia, said quite openly that it was only because of political interests that the Balkan nations painted the Ottoman Turks

---

[86] See" A history of the Indian nationalist movement", in http://www.archive.org/stream/historyofindiann00loveuoft/historyofindiann00loveuoft_djvu.txt.

". . . as cruel Asiatic tyrants, capable of European civilization. An impartial history would prove that Turks . . . are not cruel tyrants . . ."[87]

The Balkan campaign succeeded in bringing about the end of the Ottoman empire in Europe. The Ottoman empire itself was suffering from maladministration and internal factions. These, together with Balkan nationalism and the rise of European powers, were reason enough for Balkan states to take up arms against their traditional enemy, the Ottoman Turks.[88]

But it was the atrocities the conquerors committed upon Muslims under the nose of what Indian Muslims regarded was paternal Britain that seem to have stunned Indian Muslims most. Sources show Muslims had a good reason to feel bitter about their rulers. The British government had until that time fully supported the Ottoman empire. After the 1857 uprisings, the British government had persuaded the then Sultan of Turkey to issue a *fatwa* instructing Muslims to remain loyal to the British empire as part of their religious requirements. Also, the British government wholeheartedly supported the Ottoman empire during the Crimean War in 1855.

Muslims in India had come to believe in the British government as the protector of the Ottoman Sultan. One person who propagated this belief among Indian Muslims was

---

[87]   See Muhammad Momen, *Muslim India*, pp. 125-126. See also J. Howard Whitehouse, Personal Observations During the Balkan War" in The Nineteenth Century, Feb. 1913, p. 278. Also, see Charles Downer Hazen, Europe since 1815, Indian edition, 1955, pp. 567-69.

[88]   The Ottoman empire was the traditional enemy because it was the Ottoman Turks who had brought an end to the Christian Byzantine empire in 1453 C.E. Later, south-eastern Europe peoples consisting of Albanians, Greeks, Rumanians and Slavs were all subjugated under the Ottoman empire. See Ferdinand Schevill, The Balkan States and the Near East (London, 1922), p. 9.

their own compatriot, Sir Sayyid Ahmad Khan (1817-1898). After the 1857 uprisings, Sir Sayyid, a reformer, spent the rest of his life in promoting this attitude in the minds of Indian Muslims. With the defeat of the Ottoman empire at the hands of European powers, even he became anxious and is reported to have said:

> "When there were many Muslim kingdoms, we did not feel much grief when one of them was destroyed. Now that so few are we feel the loss of even small one. If Turkey is conquered that will be a great grief, for she is the last of the great power left to Islam. We are afraid we will become like the Jews, a people without a country of our own"[89]

Inside India, Muslim minds had become agitated at this turn of events. There is no doubt that Muslims had come to believe the British government to be the protector of Islam. The events that were unfolding, however, were exhibiting the opposite trend.

The events that were unfolding was activating the political consciousness among Muslims intellectuals. It was not the first time in the history of British expansion in India that Muslims rebelled. Apart from those proclaiming the Wahhabi ideology who had been rebelling now for a century, the history of the British empire in India is dotted with instances of rebellion from the time the East India Company began to exert its authority among Indians[90]." What was really new now was that for the

---

[89] Theodore Morison, "Muslim Movements" in Sir John Cumming ed. Political India 1832-1932 (London, 1932), pp. 95-96. See also Shan, *Freedom Movement in India : Role of Ali Brothers*, p. 20. See mention of this also in article by Dr. Mubarak Ali-OoCities-Geocities . . , in http://www.oocities.org/mubarak4one/mubarak/khilafat.htm.

[90] There are several examples starting from the Battle of Plassey in 1757 to the campaigns of the great Tipu Sultan in 1799 to the

very first time even the loyalists, the middle-class Muslims, on whom the British government had depended, were becoming vocal[91]. Also to be noted is that they took to religious ideology[92].

In Turkey, because of the external attack and Turkey losing its territories to the emerging European powers, and also because of the internal democratic movements associated with the *Tanzimat*[93] movements, Sultan Abdul Harnid began propagating pan-Islamic ideas. For the first time his name began to be read in Friday *khutbas* (sermons) in the mosques. We have seen in the previous chapter that according to the Hanafi school, the caliph does not have to be from the Quraysh. Indian Muslims followed the Hanafi school of law and had no problem mentioning his name in the *khutba* and referring to him as the Caliph.

Muslims in India were clearly beginning to accept the ideas of pan-Islamism, first propagated in their minds by Jamal al-Din al-Afghani (1838-1897)[94]

Jamal al-Din al-Afghani had been expelled from Egypt by Egyptian Khedive Tawfiq Pasha in 1078 because of his pan-Islamic ideas. He went to India, spending over a year in Calcutta and Hyderabad. He wrote a number of articles criticizing Sir Sayyid on various points. He totally disagreed with Sir Sayyid's views that Muslims should consider the British government to be the saviour of Islam. He opposed

---

Rebellion in 1857.

[91] "Wilfred Cantwell Smith, *Modern Islam in India*, p. 217.

[92] Ibid., p. 203.

[93] Movement for reform by Young Turks.

[94] This was an opposite trend to Sir Sayyid's teachings. At first, Jamal al-Din al-Afghani had only few disciples. It was revived only in 1912, apparently after Muslims began to perceive that the emerging European powers had an agenda to destroy the Muslim power vested in the Ottoman empire. See Smith, p. 217.

Sir Sayyid's writings on '*Ilm al-Kalam*[95] as nothing more than a heresy since it appeared to be falsifying the words of the Qur'an. Al Afghani saw Sir Sayyid's views and his educational programme as servitude to British interests in India, opposing pan-Islamism, isolating Muslims from Dar al-Islam and hostile to the Caliphate.[96]

If Sir Sayyid and Jamal al-Din al-Afghani agreed on anything, it was only that Islam was capable in adapting itself and in accord with any phase of the present and future history of mankind. Both of them wrote[97] of the need for Muslims in India to adjust themselves to modern sciences, holding that Islam encouraged this through the Qur'an and *Ahadith*, and that Muslims were themselves the pioneers of modern sciences. It is to be noted that in their writings about this, both of them followed teachings of a Tunisian scholar Khayr al-Din pasha[98]. He expressed the view that the freedom of expression brought about by Western influences should be used to bring awakening in the minds of Muslims.

Jamal al-Din al-Afghani stressed the need of the '*ulama* to arrive at the consensus of *ijtihad* [99] so that Muslims could adjust themselves in the world in which progress was in the hands of non-Muslims[100].

---

[95] This was Sir Sayyid's treatise in which he introduced theological discussion showing rational views he derived from his own interpretations on a number of issues. See Altaf Husain Hali, *Hayat-i-Javed* (Delhi: Idarah-i Adabiyat-Delli, 1979), p. 169.

[96] Ahmad, p. 54-55.

[97] Ahmad, p. 58-59.

[98] see Sir Sayyid in his *Khutut,* p. 55 andal-Afghani in his *Asbabi Haqiqati wa Sa`idati wa Shafa`ati al-Insani*, quoted by Ahmad, p.59.

[99] Ahmad, p. 60-61.

[100] he door to *ijtihad* in Sunni schools was closed, and al-Afghani is advising his readers that it should be re-opened with the 'ulama arriving at consensus to meet the needs of changing times. The first early Sunni reformer to speak about the definite need for

Thus the West became a challenge for Jamal al-Din al-Afghani, and as Wilfred Cantwell Smith tells us, al-Afghani appears to have been the first Muslim thinker who used the concept of "Islam" and "the West" as "connoting correlative"— and of course antagonistic—historical phenomena"[101]

Jamal al-Din al-Afghani was very suspicious about the motivations of the British empire[102]. He viewed the British government's subjugation of India as a dragon that had "swallowed twenty million people, and drunk up the waters of the Ganges and the Indus, but was still unsatiated and ready to devour the rest of the world and to consume the waters of Nile and Oxus".[103]

These and other ideas, coupled with the shift in the British policy towards the Ottoman empire, were bound to change the attitudes even of Muslims loyal to the British. Sources tell us[104] that a mood was emerging where Muslims felt it would have a negative effect for them if they kept borrowing from the West. It would be positive only for the Western nations as it helped increase the Western domination of Islamic lands. They wished for indigenous traditions, both Islamic and national. Jamal al-Din al-Afghani must not have been unaware of this feeling also among the Indian Muslims. He would also be aware of the

---

ijtihad was Shah Waliyullah Dahlavi (1703-1762). He argued that the door to *ijtihad* should not be closed in Islam. See Barbara Daly Metcalfe, *Islamic Revival in British India: Deoband, 1860-1900,* (Princeton: Princeton University Press), p.37. See also Ahmad, pp. 204-206. Such a need did not arise in the Shi`a school since there the doors to *ijtihad* never closed.

[101] Smith, p. 49.

[102] Quoted by Ahmad from *Taqizadeh in Mardan-i Khud-Sakht,* Teheran, 1947, p. 43.

[103] Ahmad, p. 68.

[104] See Nikki R. Keddie, *An Islamic Response to Imperialism: Political and Religious Writings of Jamal ad-Din "al-Afghani"* (Berkley: University of California Press, 1983), pp. 11-14.

Jihad movement under Shah Waliullah Dahlavi long before even the 1857 uprisings. He expressed the belief that the British government was determined to undermine Islam and substitute for it Christianity. Nikki Keddie tells us Indian Muslims believed this to be true. With the rise of Pan-Islamic ideas, we are told by William Blunt in his *India under Ripon*,[105] al-Afghani wanted to show himself the defender of Islamic orthodoxy. Al-Afghani was fully aware of the rise of the positive feeling Indian Muslims had towards the Ottoman Sultan. Keddie tells us that this trend was noted in the Government of India records, particularly after the Russo Turkish wars of 1877-1878. In 1883 al-Afghani advised William Blunt, the visiting Agent of the British government, not to upset Indian Muslims by saying anything against the Ottoman Sultan. He also advised Blunt not to say anything about the rumours circulating among Indian Muslims that the British government was planning to remove the Ottoman Caliph and replace him with an Arab[106]. If such an idea was given any weight by any British official during discussion, it would indeed be a serious matter because we are told that ever since the sixteenth century,

"Mecca had been the recognised religio-emotional centre; in the 1870's and later Istanbul took its place. A cult of Turkey developed hallowed by ideas of the caliphate, pan-Islamism and solidarity of *Dar al-Islam* against the encroaching West."[107]

Muslims in India, who had generally remained loyal to the British government[108], were now ignoring Sir Sayyid's teaching

---

[105] William Blunt, *India under Ripon* (London: 1909).

[106] There were rumours that the British government was to institute the Caliphate under a child whom they would use to make themselves the masters of the holy places. See Keddie, pp. 53ff.

[107] Ibid., p. 68.

[108] Muslims had seen clear amity between the Ottoman empire and the British empire. For example, they saw the reception the Prince of Wales (later Edward VII) received when he visited Sultan Abdul

of loyalty to the Britain and were clearly opting for loyalty to *Dar al-Islam*. They were accepting not only al-Afghani's call to pan Islamism but also his call to Muslims to recognise the Ottoman Sultan as the caliph.

In his *al-'Urwat al-wuthqa*, al-Afghani expounded ideas that became the basis of the future Khilafat movement in India. Al-Afghani said it was the religious duty of Muslims to reclaim their territory, or if this was not possible then to perform the *Hijrah* from that place because it was no longer *Dar al-Islam* but *dar al-Harb* (the abode of war). The duty to reclaim territory taken away from Muslims is a duty not limited to Muslims only of the particular territory involved. Rather, it becomes a duty for all Muslims, since Muslims everywhere are one universal body, the *Umma*. He was of the opinion that Muslim territories were conquered because there was no united resistance from Muslims everywhere. The Islamic *Umma*, to al-Afghani, had become fragmented into parts and had reduced itself to dogmas and rituals. He laid the blame squarely upon the *'ulama*. He said that this sad situation would not have arisen if the *'ulama* of various lands had not lost contact with one another. The reason for this, according to al-Afghani, was the role of the Abbasid caliphs. He said the Abbasid caliphs had separated themselves and had become a different entity from the movement of religious thought (*Ijtihad*). He pointed out this was quite contrary to the period of the four Orthodox Caliphs, and it was this dilemma that had produced sectarianism and schisms in Islam.

The situation, therefore, was that the *'ulama* needed to build up centres in each region where they could meet for discussion. They had a duty to reach out to ordinary Muslims and to guide them through using the Qur'an and the sunna as the only legitimate yardstick. Further, the regional centres should be connected directly to one universal centre. He

---

Aziz in 1868 and also the British government's support of the Ottoman empire during the Crimean War.

preferred this centre to be in one of the holy places of Islam, where the '*ulama* would meet to discuss how to revitalise the *umma* and how to meet the external challenge[109].

Jamal al-Din al-Afghani's thesis was bound to produce results among the '*ulama* in an atmosphere where Muslims had become stunned at the losses suffered by the Ottoman empire.[110] Even Sir Sayyid, towards the closing years of his life, became very anxious to see Turkey as a powerful independent Muslim State.[111] Afghani's thesis did have a desired effect. It converted a very influential '*Alim*' [112] to his camp, Maulana Shibli Nu'mani[113]. It greatly influenced the conservative stronghold in Deoband and converted Maulana Mahmud al-Hassan[114].

Another important point that al-Afghani made which touched the imaginations of Indian Muslim intellectuals was that the history of Islam was one single historical process. Therefore, any threat of subjugation of one Muslim country was a threat to all. Muslims, therefore, must not allow the division of their lands in which the European powers would install

---

[109] Ahmad quoting from Qadi 'Abd al-Ghaffar, *Ahthara-i-Jamaluddin Afghani* (Delhi, 1940), pp. 385-394.

[110] The 'ulama up to this point had generally remained loyal to the British government but this loyalty was good because of the *fatwa* that Turkey' s Sultan had pronounced after the rebellion of 1857. Now even the Sultan was propagating pan-Islamic ideas. It must be emphasised that the intellectual Indian Muslims had no particular love for Turkey other than that it represented a symbol for Islam. See Theodore Morrison, "Muslim Movements" in Sir John Cumming, ed. Political India 1832-1932 (London, 1932), pp. 95ff.

[111] See Shan Muhammad, p. 20.

[112] *Alim* is a singular form of the word 'ulama.

[113] Ikram: *Shibli Nama*, pp. 219-220.

[114] Maulana Mahmud al-Hasan was an important figure and became known as the *Shaykh al-Hind*.

petty rulers in order to keep them in bondage[115]. He thought that Muslims must have their own political centre. This, he said, would be a universal Muslim caliphate. Therefore, when Sultan 'Abdul 'Aziz began to propagate pan-Islamism, making a claim[116] that he was a universal Caliph for all Muslims everywhere, the Muslim intellectuals in India seem to have readily accepted this claim. It is interesting that al-Afghani himself had a deep distrust of the Sultan but he was too important a symbol to ignore. His distrust even led him to examine other candidates who would, to his mind, be a suitable candidate as a caliph of the Islamic umma[117]

As a result, two separate but parallel movements arose with an intent to educate and culturally reform the Indian Muslims. These movements, although politically aware, did not at first necessarily result in any political activities.[118]

The *'ulama* led a movement with the purpose of strengthening Islamic culture. The curriculum of their madrassas was reformed. Madrasas were to become important institutions since they would become a focal point for Muslims where the *'ulama* could provide their services to the public.

The second movement was led by intellectuals through the Aligarh Institute.[119] This is the institution that was originally

---

[115] see *al-'Urwat al-Wuthqa*, pp. 395-400.

[116] See W.S. Blunt, The Future of Islam, pp. 81-84.

[117] Al-Afghani thought of Egyptian Khedive, 'Abbas Hilmi but Egypt was already under the British influence

[118] Minault, p. 12.

[119] The Aligarh Institute was established by Sayyid Ahrnad Khan after the 1857 uprisings. The reason for establishing this was precisely reform according to the ideas of Sayyid Ahmad Khan. The Institute was to train Muslims in the English language and reform Muslims into accepting the British empire as the best thing that ever happened to Islam in India. Aligarh was soon to become a hotbed of political ferment during the Khilafat agitation.

set up by Sir Sayyid to promote the subjects of Western arts and science. The graduates from this Institute would have a better chance of employment in the civil service and would hopefully gain some clout and respect in the eyes of the British government.[120]

While both these movements initially started off with a view toward culturally reforming their society, they started off proclaiming loyalty to the British government. This was necessary in order to secure the Government's approval. By the first decade of the twentieth century, both the movements had turned political. The factors that contributed their precipitation into political involvement (other than the pan-Islamic ideas and external events already discussed) were all internal factors.

In April 1900, A. McDonnell, Lieutenant Governor of Uttar Pradesh, issued a decree for official use of the Hindi language. There had already been communal agitations on this issue in 1867. This move was seen by Muslims as unfair and not justified coming from the British government. We are told that

"Muslims were deeply agitated. Considered from the viewpoint of their educational needs, legal and social business and their progressive literature, and also considering the importance of maintaining the Hindu Muslim unity, this resolution seemed harmful.[121]

The British government took it as an attack on its authority and became vindictive against Nawab Muhsin al-Mulk. On 8 August 1900, a representative meeting was held, attended by a large number of Muslim representatives. This was the first political meeting that eventually managed to restore Urdu to its former status in law courts.

---

[120]   Minault, p. 12.

[121]   Jarnil-ud-din Ahmad, *Early Phase of Muslim Political Movement* (Lahore: Publishers United Ltd., 1967), pp. 66-67.

In the Indian Councils Act passed in 1892, the British government decreed that representation in the Councils should be secured not in England but in India and that such representation in the Councils would be represented by group interests. Viceroy Minto appointed a Committee in 1906 to examine further the question of constitutional reform and expressed the opinion that there was not sufficient representation of Muslims in the Council. The few that were represented were not elected by Muslims themselves. Muslims sent a delegation to see Gilbert Elliot Minto (Viceroy 1905-1910), who appreciated their concerns. The application of his principle, however, was not accepted until three years later in the Morley-Minto reforms of 1909.[122]

One of the greatest events in the history of Muslims in British India was the founding of the Muslim League in 1906. This was set up in order to:

1. protect and advance political rights and interests of Muslims in India.

2. foster understanding with and prevent hostility against other communities, particularly Hindus

3. voice the opinion that partition of Bengal would be in the interests of Muslims there[123]

Bengal had become too burdensome for the British government to manage. It consisted of an area of 189,000 square miles with a population of 78 million. At one point, it took three Lieutenant Governors to control. Curzon, the British government's Viceroy to India in 1899-1905, proposed partitioning it. If partitioned, eastern Bengal would be fully represented by Muslims, since they were in the majority. Hindus opposed this. In 1911, in spite of indications that

---

[122] Ahmad, p. 79.
[123] see Minault, pp. 18-19. Also Ahmad, pp. 80-81.

Bengal[124] would be separated, the British government gave in to Hindu agitation and revoked the partition of Bengal.[125] Here was a lesson for Muslims to learn: agitation also got results. Ahmad tells us that "The Hindu community undoubtedly looked upon this event as a major victory achieved through methods of violent agitation".[126]

Muslims were already embittered about the events in Muslim countries. With the events unfolding at home, Muslims clearly felt that the British government was siding with Hindus. They felt the revocation of partitioning of eastern Bengal was a political game played at the expense of Muslims. Several Muslim leaders spoke out against this. Muhammad Ali, in one of his addresses in 1923, said that it was hard to discover in history a more ignoble instance of betrayal in which loyalty was rewarded with deprivation. Another leader, Nawab Khwaja Salimullah of Dacca concluded from the British attitude towards Muslims in India that the annulment of the Bengal partition had all the appearances of concession to the clamours of an utterly seditious agitation. It had put a premium on sedition and disloyalty and had created an impression that the British government could be brought to its knees by defiance of constituted authority. The Nawab Viqar al-Mulk wrote a letter to his friend in which he concluded that the British government's policies towards Muslims were like an artillery which passed over the bodies of Muslims, irrespective of whether any life was left in them. Viqar felt that this was a ploy to annihilate Islam in India.[127]

Another unfortunate incident that occurred was the demolition of part of the mosque in Kanpur in 1913.

Since 1908, the British government had decided to widen certain roads in Kanpur. One such road passed by a Hindu

---

[124] Ahmad, pp. 101-107.

[125] Ahmad, p. 108.

[126] Ibid., p.108.

[127] ibid., pp. 108-109

temple and a mosque. In order to follow a straight line the authorities would have to demolish a temple. When Hindus in the Municipal board objected, the temple was left alone. The government, however, went ahead and demolished part of the mosque and said that since the part demolished was only an ablution area it could not be deemed to be sacred. Muslims were infuriated at this. The leaders made representations to the government. It appeared to Muslims that the government was stalling on the issue and decided one morning to rebuild the demolished portion themselves. The government viewed this as a serious breach. Armed units were sent in and indiscriminately opened fire, killing several Muslims, including children. The Muslims were unarmed. What made matters worse was also that this was the month of Ramadhan[128]. Muslims sent a delegation to England that was refused an audience. The reason given was at first was that the British government saw no advantage arising from such a meeting.[129] Eventually, when the British Government agreed, the government assured the

---

[128] In an interesting publication banned by the British government in the Proscribed Material I came across a one-page *khutba* given during the Kanpur trouble. The publication claims it was given to the congregation of ten thousand-strong Muslims who had gathered at the Jami Masjid on 4 Ramadan 1331 A.H. (18th August 1913). In a fiery speech Maulana Hadrat Khwaja Hasan Nizami Sahib Dahlavi aroused Muslimsf feelings towards sacrifice.

He referred to the British force as persecutors, and urged from Muslims, among other things, unity in the face of what he called persecution. The publication is entitled *Kaho Takbir* (say Allah is the Greatest) and begins with the Muslim chanting of faith, that the total Sovereignty and Greatness and Praise belongs only to Allah: *"Allahu Akbar Allahu Akbar La ilaha i l l a Allah Wallahu Akbar Allahu Akbar Walillahi al-hlamd"* (Allah is the Greatest, Allah is the greatest, There is no divinity except Allah, and Allah is the Greatest, Allah is the Greatest, and to Allah belongs all the praise). See also Shan Muhammad, *Freedom Movement in India: The Role of Ali Brothers*, pp. 40-51.

[129] Shan Muhammad, p. 23.

Muslims that the government's policy towards religious beliefs had not changed, and it agreed to restore the demolished part of the mosque. The plan of the ground level of the Mosque was raised. A passage underneath was built so that pedestrians could walk freely without disturbing the worshippers of the Mosque.[130]

Then there was the issue of the Aligarh Muslim University. Ever after Sayyid Ahmad Khan founded the Muslim Anglo-Oriental College (commonly referred to as the MAO College) in 1875, Sir Sayyid had a vision to raise its status to that of a university. After his death in 1898, the Sir Sayyid Memorial Fund was started in order to raise funds so that the College could be raised to university level. The Committee that was formed included the Agha Khan. A country-wide appeal was made, and funds started coming in.

A copy of the draft drawn by the Committee was discussed with Harcourt Butler, the education member of the Viceroy Council. Later, Butler informed the Committee that the sanction was received for the establishment of a University, provided there were enough funds and that the constitution was acceptable "in all its details" to the Government of India and the Secretary of State.

In the constitution drawn later, Muslims were to call this the Aligarh Muslim University. The University would be able to affiliate itself to other colleges throughout the country.

---

[130] In another one-page publication, government in the Proscribed Material, of (and) the Canpur Massacre, I found these lines "The Canpur massacre was as a result of revival of hope, courage and confidence among the Muslims of India on account of re-occupation of Adrianople by the Ottoman troops. The forces of liberation in India are hard at work. We will deal with the English once and for all. Meanwhile it is expected of you to educate, agitate and organise." Author not known. Proscribed material, entry no. 232.

Muslims were very excited and a large amount of money was raised. When the campaign was at its height, the committee received a letter from the British government objecting to their request for affiliation with other universities and colleges. Further, the letter said it should be called only "University of Aligarh" instead of "Muslim University of Aligarh".[131]

With these developments, Muslims in India became very agitated. People began to produce and read new anti-British poems and essays.[132] These lamented the loss of Islamic glory, or the current sufferings of Muslims and the further suffering that was still to come, they said, "at the hands of the destructive, domineering West.[133] Their works included satires, epigrams and odes[134] such as Iqbal's making a "complaint"[135] to Allah about the troubles and crisis upon crisis that have befallen

---

[131] Shan, p. 61. See also Smith and Minault.

[132] It is important to note here that the most prevalent form of expression and communication in India among the masses has always been through the medium of poems. We will see in this thesis several examples of this method of communication. This method of communication was used successfully during political agitation and also during the Pakistan movement in India. Since poetry is a form of expression that deals with emotions, this method was successfully employed to reach out to the mass of Indian Muslims who were otherwise largely illiterate. It should be noted that although poetry reaches and appeals also to the illiterate, the ability to compose extemporaneously a quick couplet or two during conversation has always been considered to be the mark of an educated and cultivated person. Some of these poems were considered seditious and were proscribed by the British government. Now released, several of these poems have been shown in this thesis for the first time.

[133] Smith, p. 128.

[134] Of these, Muhammad Iqbal' s Odes are popular in any literary talks or essays.

[135] See Smith, p. 128.

His chosen umma. His reply (shiqwa and Jawaab-i-shiqwa) is simply a masterpiece. His nostalgic Ode goes as follows:

Chino 'Arab hamara, Hindus tan hamara,
Muslim hai ham watan hai,
Sara jahan hamara.
Ay Gulistaan-i Andlus,
Woh din hay yaad tujhko,
Thaa teri daaliyon men
Jab aashiyan hamarav
(Oh those days when) China and Arabia belonged to us, Hindustan belonged to us, (and all) Muslims were compatriots. (Then) the whole earth was ours. O ye the gardens of Andalusia! Do you remember those days, When in your branches was our dwellings?

As Smith tells us, what also helped move Muslims into serious thinking and action were the four periodicals that came out.[136] These were:

The "Comrade" and "Hamdard", published by Muhammad Ali; "al-Hilal", published by Maulana Abul Kalam Azad; and The "Zamindar", published by Zafar 'Ali Khan.

Of the personalities of their publishers we are concerned with in this chapter are the first two, Muhammad Ali and Maulana Abul Kalam Azad. These two were intellectuals and knew diplomacy and how to get things done. The third, Zafar 'Ali Khan, was a "born rebel and profoundly anti-British".[137] It was becoming clear that while Sir Sayyid believed it was necessary for Indian Muslims to allow the British government to define the terms and conditions of their political life, the generation of Muslims that followed in the decade before the

---

[136] Ibid., p. 218.
[137] See Smith, pp. 218-219.

First World War were not prepared to accept colonial status of their political thought.[138]

MUHAMMAD ALI (1878-1931)

Muhammad Ali was born in 1878 and orphaned at an early age. After he was orphaned, his twenty-seven-year-old mother insisted on all her children[139] being sent to Aligarh after they completed their early education at Bareilly English School.[140] Muhammad Ali later went to England to sit for the Indian Civil Service examinations. He did not qualify but stayed on in England to complete his Honours degree in modern history at the prestigious Oxford University, where he majored in the subject of the "Rise and Fall of Muslim Powers"[141].

Once back in India, Muhammad Ali took an active part in the affairs of the Aligarh College, his alma mater. He was a good orator, and an admirer of Aligarh College. He participated in the conferences held for the proposed Muslim University. His scholarly lectures in conferences won praises, and his ideas to

---

[138] Peter Hardy, *The Muslims of British India* (Cambridge: Cambridge University Press, 1972), p. 179.

[139] The five children were four boys and one girl. The youngest two were Shaukat Ali and Muhammad Ali. We do not know much about other boys except that one (Nawazish Ali) died in infancy. The other, Zulfiqar Ali, was the eldest and completed his education early. Shaukat Ali and Muhammad Ali went to school together. Shaukat Ali made his name more on the cricket field. Muhammad Ali turned out to be the true intellectual and became a leader in the Khilafat Movement. See Shan Muhammad, pp. 2-3.

[140] Muhammad Ali s mother, Abadi Banu Begum, never re-married. She sacrificed all her personal pleasure to bringing up children fully educated. See Maulana Mohamed Ali, *My Life: A Fragment,* (Lahore, Sh. Muhamad Ashraf, 1942), pp. 5-6.

[141] Shan, p. 7.

expand Aligarh College to include engineering and technology won approval from all members.

In 1906, Muhammad Ali also took part in the formation of the Muslim League, taking part also in drafting of its constitution. He said that the time had come for Muslims to have their own separate political body" because Muslims were

"on the threshold of a political career . . . (with) its own grievances, its own aspirations . . . (and) . . . want [ing] room for expansion".[142]

Muhammad Ali made clear that by a separate political body he did not mean that Indian Muslims wanted a separate nation.[143] He compared the Indian National Congress (formed in 1885 mainly by Hindus) and the Muslim League to two trees on either side of the road but joined in their roots, fixed in the same soil and getting nourishment from the same source. The branches would meet at a height and would continue to provide shade to passers-by. By this reference he meant the soil was British, nourishment was common patriotism, trunks were two political bodies and the road was the highway to peaceful progress.[144]

Evidently seeking to serve the Muslim community, Muhammad Ali decided to take up journalism and publish a journal in which he could propagate his ideas to the Muslim mass. He launched his journal, 'The Comrade'. He later said, "The reason which so irresistibly impelled me to take up journalism was that the affairs of my community just at that

---

[142] Shan, p. 11-12.

[143] This was not a very good prediction because within twenty-four years of his speech to the Muslim League in which he declined any aspirations for a separate nation for Indian Muslims, it was in the very Muslim League the Muhammad Iqbal declared Islam to be a polity.

[144] Muhamad Ali, *My Life*, p. 35. Also Shan, p. 12. See also Minault.

juncture made it the only avenue.[145] He said that India with many religions was a "federation of faiths" and he wished to merge them in the "united faiths of India". He referred to The Comrade as belonging to "all and partisan to none". [146] He preached unity of all faiths and tried to dispel illusions that Muslims were trying to create their own nation. He said in his speeches and wrote in The Comrade that Indian Muslims had only one aspiration:

> "to work out an honourable future for their community
> amidst conditions which were growing alarming and needed
> immediate guidance to play their part worthily in the
> evolution of the political system in India".[147]

He said that Muslims were not any less patriotic than some whose patriotism seeks to exclude Muslims from all schemes of Indian nationality—it is not separatism they seek but freedom to live and fit themselves for an honourable place in Indian unity.

We see, therefore, that Muhammad Ali clearly considered himself to be the leader of the Muslim community in India. He wanted to create recognition for Muslims within the Hindu majority. This effort was good as far as it lasted, and at one time it also appeared solidified, as we shall see.

With communal violence that followed subsequently, Muslims would demand a separate nation of their own. For the time being, nevertheless, The Comrade played an active role during the Balkan wars and later during the Khilafat movement. Muhammad Ali became the leader in the Khilafat Committee, after he was interned by the British government

---

[145] 1qbal Afzal (ed.), *Selected Writings and Speeches of Muhammad Ali,* vol. 1 (Lahore), pp. 3-5.

[146] Muhammad Al i, p. 34.

[147] Muhammad Ali, p. 34. See also Shan, p. 13.

in 1915, accused of political activism.[148] It was through the Muslim League that Indian Muslims would win a separate nation for themselves.[149] Muhammad Ali himself would not live to see that. He died in 1931 while returning from the Round Table Conference held in London to decide with the British government the future of India. Muhammad Ali died in Jerusalem and is buried there.

ABUL KALAM AZAD (1880-1957)

Abul Kalam Azad was from among the *'ulama* but independent of any institution. Abul Kalam Azad was born in Mecca, where earlier his father had migrated and had married an Arab wife. The family returned to India in 1890s and settled in Calcutta. Azad, therefore, received his education in India. In

---

[148] Muhammad Ali became the most outspoken leader of the Khilafat movement in the 1920s. Apart from The Comrade, Muhammad Ali was the editor of the Urdu Hamdard. When Turkey was entering the World War I, Muhammad Ali's political views became famous in the aricle, "The Choice of Turks" he wrote in the London Times. Muhammad Ali, in the article, supported Turkey's position and its aspirations. After the internment, when Muhammad Ali was released in 1920, he led a Khilafat deputation to London and made unsuccessful representations to the Prime Minister Lloyd George and members of his cabinet. See Afzal Iqbal, Select Writings and Speeches of Maulana Mohamed Ali, vol. 1 (Lahore: Sh. Muhammad Ashraf, 1942), pp. 177-216. See also Aziz Ahmad and G.E. von Grunebaum, Muslim Self-Statement in India and Pakistan 1857-1968, pp. 12-13. See also Shan Muhammad, Freedom Movement in India : The Role of a l i Brothers (New Delhi: Associated Press, 1979), p. 86.

[149] Muhamad Ali had once said that if England desired to be the gigantic and all-pervading rulers of India, they had already done an initial mistake of educating the Indians. See Afzal Iqbal, Select Speeches and Writings of Maulana Mohamed Ali, vol. 1 (Lahore: Sh. Muhammad Ashraf, 1942), p. 12.

his youth, he studied works of Sayyid Ahmad Khan and of the Egyptian reformer Shaykh Muhammad 'Abduh (d. 1905). Since Muhamad 'Abduh was a disciple of al-Afghani, his works showed al-Afghani's influence. Azad read the journal al Manar 'Abduh published in Egypt and kept in touch with the educational ideas of the Arab world[150]

Azad was also influenced by another great *'alim*, Shibli Nu'mani, Nu'mani advised Azad to continue active as an *'alim* and to write on religious reform. In 1904, at the age of twenty-four, he produced his own journal. He called it *Lisan us-Sidq* (The Utterance of the Truth). In this journal, he wrote articles on advancement of the Urdu language and sometimes on social reform. His style of writing and his ideas appealed to the editor of one of the leading Urdu newspapers, *Vakil*. Azad was offered a position as an editor, which he accepted. He began to write in *Vakil* about events in the Ottoman empire and the Middle East. His writing displayed an influence of the writings of Rashid Rida in Middle East, especially on issues that dealt with the Caliphate.[151]

In 1912, Azad launched his famous *al-Hilal*. It is through this that he gained his popularity all over India, mainly because the style in which he articulated his ideas. He advocated complete religious reform based on the Qur'an. He invited the *'ulama* to become politically active. Azad wrote many articles that dealt with wars, with the struggle to control one's desires through *jihad* and through pilgrimage in Islam. At one point he criticized the *'ulama* for bickering among themselves and said that what the *'ulama* lacked was leadership. His views on the Ottoman empire and the Caliphate were clear: he advocated support for the Ottoman empire because it contained the office of the Caliphate. The support of all Muslims was essential because the caliph was the guardian of holy places of Islam.

---

[150] Minault, p. 39. See also *Azad ki Kahani*, pp. 190-192.
[151] Albert Hourani, *Arabic Thought in the Liberal Age 1798-1939*, pp. 226-44.

Azad wrote extensively about the Balkan wars. He also encouraged other authors to compose verses and odes regarding Tripolitanian and Balkan wars. These made *al-Hilal* extremely popular.[152] Azad believed that since the Ottoman caliph was the guardian of the holy places, support for Turkey meant support for Islam. He appealed for Turkish relief and for Red Crescent funds. The emotional appeal al-Hilal contained meant expansion of its circulation but with more readership of *al-Hilal,* also more Muslims were gaining political awareness.

In his temperament, Azad is shown in sources to be impatient with those whom he did not consider to be at par with himself. He showed a general dislike of westernized Muslims. But at the same time, he recognised that the westernized Muslims affiliated with Aligarh were politically more active. He shared with Muhammad Ali similar issues relating to Islamic politics during the Balkan wars to the time of the Khilafat movement.[153]

THE *'ULAMA*

Apart from the activists, the other sector that was showing active tendencies to reform were the traditional *'ulama*. Their efforts manifested in two madrassas, the Deoband School and the Firangi Mahal.

The Deoband School was founded to chart a reformed traditional curriculum for Muslims. It was founded ten years after the uprisings against the British government, in 1867. The founders were all former students of the Delhi Madrassa of Shah Waliyullah Dahlavi (1703-1762), an eighteenth-century reformer. During the 1857 uprising, Shah Waliyullah Dahlavi's madrassa buildings were totally destroyed. The new generation reestablished the school in a mosque at Deoband. It soon grew

---

[152] Minault, pp. 38-45.
[153] See Minault, pp. 38-45.

into a complete madrassa. Three Maulanas, Muhammad Qasim Nanotavi (d. 1879), Rashid Ahmad Gangohi (d. 1905) and Zulfiqar Ali, ran this school. They modelled it on the English system, complete with departments, syllabi, examinations and finally the conferring of degrees upon graduation.[154]

The Deoband School reached out to the community at large by establishing an information service centre on Shari'a practice called *Dar al-Ifta* (abode of *Fatwa*)[155] and by promoting Urdu religious literature. It also reached out to them by seeking their participation in it and by taking contributions from them. It was begun as strictly apolitical and independent of seeking funds from any government agency.[156]

A very interesting phenomenon at this time (i.e. after the1857 uprisings) was developing in India. Since the Deoband school had reforming tendencies, it had no objection towards those Muslims who were turning away from the traditional curriculum towards education provided by Aligarh in English. There was no opposition also to acquiring knowledge in modern sciences. Deoband, it was recognised, was providing and preserving the traditional sciences without condemning those who were acquiring new knowledge elsewhere. Aligarh,

---

[154] See Sayyid Mahbub Razvi, *Tarikh-i Deoband*, pp. 110-116. See also Barbara Daly Metcalf, *Islamic Revival in British India: Deoband, 1860-1900* (Princeton: Princeton University Press, 1982), pp. 87ff.

[155] By establishing this department, the school could reach out to the public at large for all the questions regarding the daily Shari'a matters. For example, if a Muslim had a question relating to his daily life and did not know what was the correct way to go about fulfilling the required steps, he or she could ask through the Imams at this school. This related to all aspects of life, including solemnizing marriages, how to wash a dead body, rules for burials and the like.

[156] See Ziaul Hasan Faruqi, *The Deoband School and Demand for Partition*, pp. 25ff.

meanwhile, was providing Western education for Muslims who desired positions in the government and professional offices.[157]

If there was any contrast between the two, it lay in their founding principles. Aligarh was founded by Sir Sayyid, who was ferociously loyal to the British government and therefore opposed to the Indian National Congress, founded in 1885. Deoband, on the other hand, founded by the *'ulama*, issued a *fatwa* (decree) under Maulana Gangohi in which he said it would not be against the tradition of the Prophet if Muslims were to cooperate with Hindus in order to get concessions from the British government, provided they did not violate the basic tenets of Islam.[158]

The change in the Deoband School came after the death of Nanotavi in 1880, followed later by Gangohi in 1905. The position of Principal devolved upon Maulana Mahmud al-Hasan, a favourite student of Maulana Gangohi. Mahmud al-Hasan was to emerge later in the history of Indian Muslims as the *Shaykh al-Hind*, because of his political struggles against the British government. The position of head administrator was given to Maulana Hafiz Muhammad Ahmad, son of Maulana Nanotavi. There was a great difference between these two. While Mahmud al-Hasan was an activist, Hafiz Ahmad was an administrator loyal to his father's (Nanotavi) ideas. For the next fifteen years factionalism in the Deoband school based

---

[157] Generally, Muslims in the beginning remained aloof from acquiring education through the English medium. The founding of the MAO College in Aligarh, therefore, was a revolutionary step by Sayyid Ahmad Khan. Many conservative Muslims turned away from him. Up to 1857, the medium of education in India, for both Muslims as well as Hindus, was in Urdu and Persian. Shan, p. 3. See also Minault, p. 26.

[158] 1bid. Also see Maulana Sayyid Muhammad Mian, *'Ulama-i Haq aur Un Ke Mujahidanah Karname*, vol. 1 (Moradabad: Kutubkhana Fakhriya, 19481, p. 98.

on loyalties of the two became an important factor.[159] Maulana Mahmud al-Hasan reached out to the community of Muslims at large by organising two associations. One was the association of Deoband graduates who would reach out to other Muslims. He called this association the *Jami'at al-Ansar* (Community of Helpers). The other association was directed at those who received their education in English but did not have opportunity to enrol themselves in the study of Islamic traditions. This was called *Nazarat al-Ma'tifat al-Qur aniyya* (Study of the Qur'anic Sciences) and through it Qur'anic schools were established in Delhi.

Maulana Mahmud al-Hasan took in with him an old student of his, Maulana 'Ubaydullah Sindi, a Sikh convert to Islam. Sindi drafted a pamphlet showing the objectives of the *Jami'at al-Ansar*. The draft showed reforms based on the teachings of Shah Waliyullah Dahlavi, public speaking and writing. The draft was recommended for branches all over the country. The *ulama* therefore would be visible everywhere in the country to advise Muslims regarding their religious and legal questions.[160]

These kinds of reforms were bound to make the administrators of the school nervous because they saw in these reforms political objectives. Maulana Hafiz Ahmed, who as we have already seen was loyal to his late father's ideas, decided to deal with this problem by nipping it in the bud. He issued a *fatwa* declaring Sindi to be an infidel.[161] Mahmud al-Hasan sent Sindi to Delhi to start a Qur'an school in Delhi.

Mahmud al-Hasan's second association, *Nazarat al-Ma'rifat al-Qur'aniyya* (pondering the gnosis of the Qur'an) was designed to instruct English-educated Muslims about Islam and also to increase the influence of the *ulama*. As we have seen,

---

[159] Minault, p. 27. Also see Madni's Naqsh-i-Hayat, vol. 1, pp. 131 ff.

[160] See Rahman, *Tazkira*, p. l53 ff.

[161] Husain Ahmad Madni, *Naqsh-i-Hayat,* 2 vols. (Deoband : Maktaba-i Diniya, 1953-1955), 1: 144.

when Ubaydullah Sindi was fired from Deoband, he was sent by Mahmud al-Hasan to Delhi to start a Qur'an school there. Sindi set up the school in Old Delhi. Soon this school included patrons also from Aligarh, including Muhammad Ali. Included also were Abul Kalam Azad and Dr. Mukhtar Ahmad *Ansari*. It was Dr. *Ansari* who led later a Red Crescent mission to Turkey in 1912.

In an interesting source that deals with the Indian Muslims in British India, we are told that although Iqbal and Abul Kalam Azad and the *'ulama* would disagree on how "the Holy Law of Islam was to be interpreted and applied in the twentieth century or indeed who was to interpret it, they were atone in rejecting the secular territorial state and a political life founded upon western assumptions".[162]

With the outbreak of the Tripolitanian and Balkan wars, followed by World War I, the *'ulama* of Deoband became increasingly concerned about the fate of the Caliphate. With this development, it seemed that Indian Muslims would become more politically active.

It is worth noting that Mahmud al-Hasan did not engage himself in political activities in India. He sought Muslim allies outside India and indulged in activities across the Afghan border. This would eventually land him in the Silken Letters Conspiracy and internment in Malta all through the World War I.[163]

---

[162] See Peter Hardy, *The Muslims of British India*, p. 180.

[163] In 915, Mahmud al-Hasan left India, saying he was going for the Hajj pilgrimage to Makka. In fact it was alleged by the British government that he had arranged with Ubaidullah Sindhi, who had slipped out of India earlier to Afghanistan, to set up a base of operations there. The plan was to invade India from Afghanistan using Turkish aid. The correspondence between al-Hasan and Ubaidullah was carried by sympathisers. These messages were written on silk and sewn into the under-garments or the lining of their coats. One of these synpathisers was caught. Mahmud

FIRANGI MAHAL

Unlike the Deoband School, Firangi Mahal[164] had a long history. It came not existence in the reign of Mughal emperor Aurangzeb (1658-1707). The early *'ulama* made it an extremely successful school. Their famous curriculum, *Dars-i-Nizamiyya* (the Nizamiyya Syllabus), was named after the early Maulana from the school's founding generation, Mulla Nizamuddin.

In the twentieth century, this curriculum was still in operation teaching Arabic, *mantiq* (logic), *falsafa* (philosophy), and *fiqh* (jurisprudence).[165]

The Firangi Mahal at the turn of the century was run by Maulana Abdul Bari (1878-1926) of Firangi Mahal. He was from the *'ulama* and belonged to two Sufi orders at the same time, the *Qadi*ri and the Chishti orders.

Abdul Bari decided in 1905 to undertake reforms, He decided to raise the status of Dars-i-Nizamiyya from a traditional madrassa to an institution where the westernized Muslims could also learn the recitation and the commentary of the Qur'an. Abdul Bari was helped mainly by his own family.

---

al-Hasan was blamed for this. see *Mian*, 1: 139. See also *Naqsh*, 2: 137-43.

[164] This was established at the turn of the eighteenth century. Firangi Mahal was, in fact, Mughal emperor Aurangzeb's gift to the children of one of his loyal patrons, Mulla Qutb al-Din (d.1691/2) who had helped in collecting for the emperor his Fatawa-i 'Alamgiri. Firangi Mahal was always known as such ever since it was built first by a French adventurer. See Barbara Metcalf, pp. 29-30. Such names are not uncommon in the Indo-Pakistan sub-continent. *Firang*i comes from the Arabic word *faranj* (frank) meaning a European and *mahal*, also from Arabic, is an Urdu word meaning Mansion. (In Hindi, it would be Firangi Bhavan, much the same as India's several Mueller Bhavans, named after Max Mueller).

[165] Minault, pp. 32-33. See also Mujeeb, Indian Muslims, p. 407.

The Firangi Mahal included also the two brothers, Maulana Abdul Majid and Abdul Hamid. Both resigned from their posts and accused Abdul Bari of political activism; (since) both were in the government camp[166]. The British government, showing their appreciation to their sympathisers, gave them a grant of 3000 rupees to start up a competitive school near the Firangi Mahal. This clearly indicated that the British government thought of Abdul Bari as a dissident. As for Abdul Bari, the British government's hostility towards the Ottoman empire during the war, and at home setting up for the two Abduls the rival school only intensified their anti-government feelings. Abdul Bari had also come in contact with other politically active westernised Muslims. This included Muhammad Ali, Shaukat Ali, Dr. Mukhtar Ahmad Ansari and Abul Kalam Azad.

During discussion with the Ali brothers, Abdul Bari suggested a need to form an association to protect the holy places of Islam from harm. There were rumours that Italy was planning to bomb the holy places of Islam. The reason to form an association to prevent Italy or any other government from bombing holy places, Abdul Bari felt, was that the Ottoman empire had grown too weak to defend them by itself. It was therefore the duty of all Muslims everywhere to join the defense.

The Ali brothers, very impressed with Abdul Bari's approach and his fervor to unite Muslims and provide help in the cause of Islam. They agreed to send relief aid to Turkey and also to from the *Anjuman-i-Khuddam-i-Ka`ba*. Abdul Bari helped Ali brothers read and understand the Qur'an in Urdu.[167]

An association was formed, calling itself *Anjuman-i- Khuddami-Ka'ba* (society of the servants of the Ka'ba). It was decided

---

[166] Minault, p.34.

[167] Minault, p. 35.

to seek membership of Muslims all over India.[168] Funds would be raised to help ensure the safety of the holy places of Islam and also to help pilgrims going to these places. The association proclaimed this was only for religious reasons, and had nothing to do with politics.[169] They began to mobilise. Branches were opened throughout the major centres of India.[170] The word Anjuman became a household word as it was mentioned in the *khutbas*, leaflets, printed notices and in Urdu journals. Every city, town and village throughout India had its own local unit. Included in the whole India were also the princely states. All seemed to have endorsed this organization.[171] Abdul Bari also produced an open letter asking for the support to their cause.[172] Monies were also raised asking from Muslims their zakat tax.[173]

---

[168] Bombay, Dacca, Hyderabad and Lucknow. Besides these important centres, local branches were opened in Punjab and Uttar Pradesh. See Minault, p. 36. Every Muslim, male or female, could enrol as the *khadim* (servant) of the Ka'ba and had to take an oath: "I . . . son (or daughter) of . . . believing Allah to be Omnipresent and Omniscient, asking forgivenesss for my sins, and reciting the "Formula of Testimony" 'I bear witness that there is no god but Allah and I bear witness that Muhammad is His Servant and His Messenger, and standing with my face towards the Ka'ba, sincerely affirm that I will heartily endeavour to preserve the sanctity of the Ka'ba (pointing towards it) from violation, and, in the event of a non-Moslem attack on the Ka'ba, will not spare my life or my property, and will, in all particulars, follow the orders and rules of the Society of the Servants of the Ka'ba if Allah willeth." See Shan, p. 75.

[169] Minault, p. 35.

[170] Bombay, Dacca, Hyderabad and Lucknow. Besides these important centres, local branches were opened in Punjab and Uttar Pradesh. See Minault, p. 36.

[171] Shan, p. 75-76.

[172] See M. Inayatullah, *Hasrat al-Afaq ba Vafat-e-Majmua al-Akhlaq*, pp. 11-13.

[173] The religious tax (two and one-half percent) levied upon those who have money as savings. It is alms-giving which could be used through proper *fatwa* in the defence of Islam.

During discussions, some seemingly incredible proposals were put forward by members. These included to buy their own airplanes and to present them to the Turkish military; or to build up a Muslim fleet or give a dreadnought to Turkish navy. For helping pilgrims, the purchase of a Muslim-owned steamship was proposed. The ship would provide transportation for pilgrims between Bombay and Jedda.[174]

Thus, the Firangi Mahal and the *Anjuman-i-Khuddam-i-Ka'ba*, brought about alliance of the *'ulama* and the western-educated intellectuals. For the propagation of their ideology to the Muslim masses, the Anjuman promoted religious symbols like the Ka'ba, Medina, the Caliph, the crescent and the green robes that they wore. These symbols aroused all Muslims, men and women, educated and illiterate alike.

The alliance between the *'ulama* and westernised Muslims, together with the Russo-Turkish and Balkan wars, brought about among Muslims a spirit or movement of nationalism. Muslim papers called for the boycott of European goods. Political speeches became rampant. Students engaged in swadeshi (nationalist) activities. In the Kanpur (Cawnpore) Mosque incident of 1913, as we saw earlier, several lives were lost as the police opened fire, but these incidents also taught Muslims that with persistence and unity, positive results could be achieved.

Then came the First World War. To Muslims, this war was being fought not only to further the aims of the colonizing powers, but more importantly against the only remaining Muslim power, the Ottoman empire.[175] The most natural

---

[174] Muhammad Ali produced a letter in which he outlined the services the Anjuman was determined to provide to the pilgrims. See Ali, *My Life,* pp. 48-50. See also Minault, p. 3

[175] It is noteworthy that during the war the Indian Muslim pilgrims to Makka and Madina kept a diary of events that occurred in Makka and Madina. Later, in 1921, during the height of the Khilafat and

thing for the British government to do was to assure Muslims immediately that the real war aims did not include harm to holy places. Britain was also not against the institution of the Caliphate. The war was one in which, in the words of the official declaration published by the government of India in November 1914, and officially circulated in every town and village in India:

"The Musselmans of India should rest assured that nothing will be done by us or by our allies in this war which is likely to injure their feelings and sentiments. The holy places of Islam shall remain immune from molestations and every care will be taken to respect them. No operation will be conducted against the sacred seat of the Muslim Khilafat, we are only fighting the Turkish ministers who are acting under the influence of Germany and not the Khalifa of Islam. The British government not only on their behalf but also on behalf of their allies takes the responsibility of all these pledges".[176]

The proclamation is indeed very reassuring when we read it even now. Muslims, on the whole, accepted the pledge from the British government as genuine. But with leaders interned

---

the non-cooperation movements, their writings were published and were immediately proscribed. What is unique about their diary is that they compared the war and the siege of Madina with the Karbala event. Their article appeared under the title, 'Horrified Events Like Karbala, *un Karbala Numa Qiyamat*. They wrote, "This is the revelation of that horrifying events resembling nothing less than Karbala that occurred in Makka . . . The treachery of the Shariff of Makka . . . made possible the siege of Madina and the horrifying bombardments from air . . . Ib See Proscribed Material, entry number 1445, *Khun-i Haramayn: Un Karbala Numa Qiyamat*. See appendix 1.

[176] Syed Mahmud, *Khilafat and England*, p. 5. See also http://www.amazon.it/The-Khilafat-England-Classic-Reprint/dp/B008N6H3TO and "Jinnah, Khilafat and RSS-Scribd" in http://www.scribd.com/doc/39243063/Jinnah-Khilafat-and-RSS.

and periodicals suppressed, in some quarters anxiety set in. In the Punjab, the rural population, fed up with the economic chaos that the country was faced with during the war, started the Ghadr movement (1914-1915). This movement was fiercely put down by the government but it did stir up the population, which though not necessarily Muslim, was willing to join any movement of protest.[177]

Another group that showed its protest were some devout Muslim soldiers who deserted the British army to avoid fighting against their fellow Muslims. Those that did not desert found themselves with very low morale having to fight against their own Muslim brothers.

Then there were conservative Muslims. They began to see the pledges given by the British government in a different light. To them, the British empire's instigation that led to the Arab revolt,[178] their active campaigning in Mesopotamia to sow sedition against the Ottomans, and the fall of Jerusalem, were enough reasons to feel apprehensive about the real intentions of the British empire. To make things even worse, the transportation difficulty faced by the pilgrims to Makkah during the war and the Balfour declaration following the fall of Jerusalem certainly added to their anxieties.

Muslims began to register their protest through the Friday *khutbas* in the mosques. The caliph's name began to appear in Friday sermons with special prayers for the caliph and

---

[177] Smith, P. 220.

[178] This was the revolt against the Ottoman empire skillfully instigated by T.E. Lawrence, a young British scholar who joined the British army and was assigned with the task of gathering intelligence information. T. E. Lawrence s involvement led to an alliance of Arab tribes. The Muslim League in India passed a resolution declaring the Sharif of Mecca, Husayn ibn 'Ali (greatgrandfather of the present King Abdullah of Jordan) the enemy of Islam.

the preservation of the Ottoman empire.[179] The Ali brothers maintained contacts with the outside world. They were impressed with Mohandas K. Gandhi, who had returned from South Africa and almost immediately plunged himself into Indian politics to lead a movement against the British Raj. They heard him speak and liked his statement that politics and religion always go hand in hand and cannot be divorced.[180]

Also, there was a growing friendship and cooperation between the Indian National Congress and the Muslim League. Muhammad Ali Jinnah clearly saw the tremendous influence that could be wielded in demanding certain rights from the British empire if there were a unity between the Congress and the League. His efforts led to the Lucknow Pact, signed in their joint meeting in Lucknow in 1916.[181]

Jinnah's success in bringing together the League men with the Congressmen made him an official spokesman for Muslims, especially when the Muslim League supported another activist who had demanded Home rule, the Theosophist Annie Besant. Annie Besant was interned, too. Jinnah spoke against the internment.

With these developments in India, the British government in 1917 announced through the Secretary of State for India, Montague, that it was considering gradual self-government that would eventually become a responsible government in India and would remain as an integral part of the British empire. Montague made a special trip to India to observe the direct

---

[179] Maulana Muhammad Ali with this brother Maulana Shaukat Ali, although interned, were still free in their movements and could go to the Friday prayers in the Mosques. They had become symbol of struggle against what muslims in India saw as foreign powers meddling with the domination of the Muslim Ottoman empire.

[180] see Khaliquzzaman, *Pathway to Pakistan*, p. 33. Also see D.G. Taluqdar, *Mahatma*, vol. 1. 161ff.

[181] See Minault, p. 56.

reaction to his announcement by Indians themselves. He was enthusiastically met by several delegations from different groups. The joint Congress-League requested Montague to recognise the Lucknow Pact officially. When Annie Besant was released in 1917, she called for the release of the Ali brothers as well. The British government would release the Ali brothers if they would give the undertaking the Government asked. It demanded from the Ali brothers a signed statement that they would not support enemies of the empire (i.e., the Ottoman empire) and would not attempt to instigate violent agitation against the government. The Ali brothers agreed but said that they could not be restricted to observe their religious aspirations as Muslims. The government understood they meant to continue voicing their opinions in favour of the Ottoman empire and particularly its caliph. They were refused freedom. The Muslim League had elected Muhammad Ali as the president of the League that year.[182] Nevertheless, they graced the empty presidential chair of the League during their session that year by placing Muhammad Ali's s photograph on it. They also asked his mother, Bi Amman, to speak on behalf of her son. While remaining veiled, Bi Amman, gave a stirring speech.[183]

Then came the communal riots in 1917 and 1918. These gave rise to enormous anxieties. Muslims began to feel unsafe even in India. It was not that communal hatred between Muslim and Hindu communities had not existed before. It was the timing of the riots: during the 'Eid al-Adha, when Muslims sacrificed cows as charity to feed the poor, and during the commemoration of Muharram, when Muslims remembered and mourned the 'Ashura tragedy sacrifices in Karbala[184] of the

---

[182] Muslims had anticipated release of the Ali brothers.

[183] See Minault, p. 58.

[184] The he timing of the riot on the 'Ashura day in the month of Muharrarn brought all Muslims together. While in the rest of the Muslim world, the 'Ashura day event is mainly commemorated by the Shi'as, it is unique in India that both the Sunni as well

grandson of the Prophet. Muslims viewed the situation very seriously. They felt totally isolated by what they perceived to be threats to their cherished faith both internally (from Hindus) and externally (from the British empire and its allies).

But this emotion represented for the political leaders an important opportunity. It had an energy so potent that it could be harnessed for any purpose the leaders wished. One important development was that the moderate leaders were losing ground. This was understandable because with the communal violence and defeat of the Ottoman empire, moderate leaders were not considered as leaders with vision. A clear swing of power was occurring from moderates to those with a hard line. Also, when Montague-Chelmsford was made

---

as theShi`a communities join in. The reasons for Shi`a and Sunni to be united in Muharram are not difficult to see. First, Muslims were a minority in India. Muslim poets of India always used the Muharram event to refer to Muslims as one body placed in a situation where as minority were suffering both under the hands of the British as well as the Hindus. Second, many Mughal emperors had special friendship treaties with their cousin neighbours, the Saf avids in Iran, who had almost simultaneously with the Mughal empire set up their own dynasty. The Safavids were Shi`as who had in their palaces Sunni wives. Likewise, the Mughal emperors had Shi`a wives in their palaces. Nurjahan herself, in whose memory the emperor Shahjahan built the famous Taj Mahal, was a Shi`a herself. Moreover, most Mughal emperors supported the Muharram commemoration of the Karbala event, and in some cases, took part in the processions themselves. They evidently saw in the Muharram commemoration, a unifying force in their subjects. They supported them perhaps also because they did not want to be branded by their subjects as despots like Yazid. We shall see later that Muharram played a major role in uniting Muslims in their demand for Pakistan because they compared the majority Hindu rule, in which they could foresee no social justice for Muslims, with that of Yazid ibn Mu'awiya.

public, the report did not recognize the Lucknow Pact that the League men had worked so hard to achieve.

In order to harness this energy, a united Muslim front was needed. As we have seen thus far, it did not really exist. We have seen that Muslim consciousness had risen. Muslims were more aware, whether they came from the madrasas or whether from Western educational institutions such as Aligarh. What really provided this link was the threat with the defeat of the Ottoman empire, the fate of the Caliphate. This link was provided by the 'ulama as their concerns over the Caliphate merged with the concerns of Muslims at all other levels. To the 'ulama, the institution of the Caliphate was a religious symbol required to be maintained in Shari'a. To the intellectual Muslims, the Caliphate became a symbol of religious freedom; and of wartime promises, specifically liberation and self-administration, the British government had given to the colonised peoples. To the ordinary Muslims, the Caliphate was a symbol with many meanings. It meant to them, all the above but also, as Pandit Jawaharlal Nehru put it, a chance to oppose the authority (taken from the word khilaf which meant in Urdu "to oppose")[185]

Although the 'ulama provided the link, it was only after the 'ulama had their own meeting at the Fatehpur Sikri Mosque where they discussed their ideas and concerns vis-a-vis the ideas presented by the intellectuals. They agreed that their role as the spiritual leaders included guiding Muslims in all aspects of their lives, including politics. The 'ulama were later invited to attend the December 1918 annual Muslim League session. There the 'ulama spelt out their concerns. They asked the intellectuals not to think that politics was their realm whereas religion that of the 'ulama. Rather, in Islam, politics and religion are fused together and are inseparable. Also, they made clear

---

[185] See Jawharlal Nehru, An Autobiography (Delhi : Allied Press, 1962), p. 226. See also Minault, p. 59ff.

that in the time of danger it was the duty of the *'ulama* not to sit idle but to play a leading role.

Resolutions were passed that became the prelude to the Khilafat movement in India. Among the resolutions passed were:

1. the principle of self-determination as outlined in the war aims,

2. the sanctity of Muslim holy places and the withdrawal of all armed forces from the Hijaz, Damascus, Baghdad, Najaf and Karbala,

3. decision on the question of the Caliphate to be made only by Muslims, who shouid be given full religious freedom, and

4. the release of internees.

With these resolutions, the *'ulama* joined in. The Ali brothers again sought in 1918 to be released but their appeal was to no avail because of the war. As a result they became special heroes in India. When they were finally released in 1919, they were in time for the League session. Muhammad Ali arrived not only triumphant, but as an unopposed leader of the Khilafat movement that was about to be launched.

The Khilafat movement was an issue that touched Hindus as well. It was of concern to Hindus because it was an issue that was clearly anti-British. If only they could unite with Muslims, a mass movement would be possible. Gandhi would see this and would launch a movement that would for the first time unite Hindus and Muslims, chanting *Hindu-Muslim bhay-bhay* (Hindus and Muslims, brothers unto one another). This would change the face of Indian nationalism, forever. We shall look at this issue and the movement itself in the next chapter.

CHAPTER THREE:

THE BEGINNING AND THE ORGANIZATION OF THE KHILAFAT MOVEMENT

We saw in the previous chapter that by the beginning of the twentieth century, Muslims in India had their political consciousness considerably aroused. From among the several factors, we saw the main reason for this was that the British government had stopped supporting the Ottoman empire. While the British government might have withdrawn its support for the Ottoman empire because of its own strategic interests, Muslims clearly felt the reason was the British government's deliberate policy to weaken the power of Islam in Europe. This in turn left Muslims with two choices: whether to continue feeling the same loyalty they had towards the British government or to accept the theory introduced by Jamal al-din al-Afghani of *Dar al-Islam*.

Muslims felt the British government, which they had come to regard as saviour of Islamic power in the world, had abandoned them. They felt this way because of several incidents that took place. Among these were the British government's attitude towards the Ottoman empire during Tripolitanian and Balkan wars, the annulment of partition of Bengal, the Kanpur Masjid incident and the failure of the Muslim university of Aligarh movement. Muslims became united in accepting the theory of *Dar al-Islam*. In doing so, they were adopting Jamal al-Din al-Afghani's political ideology of pan-Islamism at the expense of Sir Sayyid's solemn pledge for Muslims in India to remain reverently devoted and loyal to the British government.

In one of his articles, Sir Sayyid had written,

"We are devoted and loyal subjects of the British government. We are not the subjects of Sultan Abdul Hamid II [for] he [does not have and never can have] any spiritual jurisdiction over us as Khalifa.[186]

Sir Sayyid did not believe that Muslims in India, if given choice, would ever adopt, other status except than loyal British subjects. In his work, *Truth about Khilafat*[187] he assured the British government that Muslims were enjoined in their religion to be loyal to their rulers. In his mind, Muslims could never be aroused to support Turkey because of the Turk's own administrative weakness that caused revolts against them in Herzegovina, Syria and Crete[188].

Sir Sayyid' s views were increasingly coming under attack, even from his contemporaries. By 1906, even Muhsin al-Mulk, who had supported Sir Sayyid's views, turned away from such ideas[189]

As we have already seen, political realities of the day were bringing Muslim intellectuals and the *'ulama* together. Aligarh's achievement under Sir Sayyid were being questioned. *Nadwat al-'ulama* had become Aligarh's anti-thesis rather than its complement.[190] The vast majority of Muslims in India were turning their thoughts instead to the *Dar al-Islam* and

---

[186] Sayyid Ahmad Khan, *Aakhiri Mazamin*, p. 323. See also "Writings and Speeches of Syed Ahmad Khan", http://dart.columbia.edu/library/DART-0050/DART-0050.pdf.

[187] Khan, *Truth about Khilafat* (Lahore, 1916).

[188] Even with these views Sayyid Ahmad conceded that Muslims had sympathy towards the Ottoman empire as a last surviving Muslim power.

[189] Smith, p. 30.

[190] Aziz Ahmad, Sayyid Ahmad Khan, "Jamal al-Din Afghani and Muslim India" in Studica Islamica (1960), pp. 73ff.

more finding Jamal al-Din al-Afghani's pan-Islamism most appealing. As the *'ulama* found support among Muslim masses, the madrasas became active with ideas of pan-Islamism. Even Aligarh, traditionally loyal to the British government, revolted under Muhammad Ali forcing its funds collected to convert the Muslim Anglo Oriental College into a Muslim university to be invested in Turkish government bonds.[191]

Al-Afghani had spelled out in his *al 'Urwat al-Wuthqa* certain ideas that would become the basis of the Khilafat movement in India. According to al-Afghani, Muslims had a duty to reclaim their territory. If reclaiming was not possible, it meant Muslims would live in *Dar al harb* (as opposed to *Dar al-Islam*) and should therefore do a *hijrah*[192]. Muslim communities were not restricted to any one particular region. Rather, they were part of the whole body. Therefore, if Muslims in Turkey were affected, it was the duty of Muslims all over to feel the pain.[193]

By the end of the War, almost all Muslims had come to accept Jamal al-Din al-Afghani's pan-Islamic theory.

Another factor which turned Muslims more towards Pan-Islamism was that Muslims began to fear for their future among Hindus because of the inter-communal violence that had erupted in the preceding years.

---

[191] Ibid., p. 73.

[192] *Hijra* smply means migration to another place more suitable for one to live, practise and propagate Islam. Jamal al-Din al-Afghani's theory stated that if Muslims were not able to recover their territory lost to the British government in India then for them India became *Dar al-Harb* (abode of war). They should then migrate to other lands. This was put into practice by thousands of Muslims during the Khilafat agitation, as we shall see.

[193] Undoubtedly, Jamal al-Din al-Af ghani took support in this from the famous Hadith recorded in many sources. The Prophet is recorded to have said that the whole of the Muslim *umma* is one body. If any part of the body hurts, the whole body suffers pain.

In the conduct of the British government they saw the Montagu-Chelmsford reforms not adopted in their entirety. Then, the defeat of the Ottoman empire at the hands of the Allied forces was a blow very hard to endure.

The other factors that produced general discontent among all Indians were economic and social. During the war, the prices of commodities rose considerably. The hardest hit economically were mainly Muslims, since from the time of 1857 uprisings, they were denied equal opportunities in government jobs compared with Hindus. Muslims were very slow in accepting the reality that, as we have already seen in ch. 2, the Mughal empire had finally been wiped out from the face of India. Muslims had neither accepted the abolition of the Shari'a courts nor had they accepted the abolition of Urdu as the main language of teaching and communication in India.[194] Muslims had become afraid for the Islamic power in the world.

By 1918, it had become amply clear that the situation prevailing in the minds of Muslims needed new political initiatives. Those who were constitutionally minded among them knew that this discontent could be mobilised to broaden their own constituencies. There was an enormous potential in this discontent so that a Muslim constituency could be used as an important component and expand it to the national movement. Gandhi, too, knew this. In my view, as we shall see later, Gandhi would eventually unite Hindus with Muslims and turn this discontent in the Khilafat movement into a national movement. Gandhi was helped in this also because of economic factors. Food prices spiraled in the years 1918-1919 because of no monsoon rains. Also, there was the eruption of an influenza

---

[194] Initially, as the British rule spread, the English language was seen replacing the Persian language. See Anil Seal, *The Emergence of Indian Nationalism* (Cambridge : CambridgeUniversity Press, 1968). pp. 300-305. Persian still remained the language of law in the shari'a courts. By the nineteenth century, the main language of daily communication in India was undoubtedly Urdu.

epidemic which brought great difficulties for the Indian population as a whole. Gandhi and the Muslim leaders could clearly see that the whole of the Indian population had very little confidence left in the economic and social policies Mass political agitation threatened to erupt and Gandhi, it seemed, would get his chance to unite Hindus with Muslims. Gandhi's chance came after the government forced the hurried passage of the Rowlatt Bills in the Legislative Council. The reason why it was felt necessary to pass the Rowlatt Bills through the Legislative Council. The British government saw a very strong anti-British strategy being planned in which even the foreign governments (Germany, Russia and the Ottomans) would take part to wage a war against the British in India.

Known later as "The Silk Letters", the plan originated from the Deoband seminary under Ubaidullah Sindi and Shaykh Mahmud al-Hasan.[195] We saw in Ch.2. that they founded in the Deoband Seminary Jami'at dl-*Ansar* in 1909 with a view to propagate anti British feeling throughout India. Following the Kanpur Masjid incident in 1913, Ubaidullah Sindi and Mahmud al-Hasan held a belief that India had become for Muslims Dar al-Harb. They planned for Mahmud al-Hasan to go to Makkah and enlist the support of the Sharif of Makkah to wage a war against the British through the North West Frontier in Afghanistan. The whole plan was written down; in it was revealed that support would come also from the German and Turkish mission. The letters were intercepted at the border crossings[196] This led the British government to pass the Rowlatt bills under the Defence of India Act. This move was condemned both by Hindus and Muslims alike. Mass demonstrations

---

[195] See Mian, pp. 139-142. See also Ziya-ul-Hasan Faruqi, *The Deoband School and The Demand for Pakistan* (Bombay: Asia Publishing House, 1963), pp. 59 ff.

[196] The Silken Letter plan might not have failed if it had been organised and planned properly. See Adamec Ludwig, *Afghanis tan, l9OO-923* (Berkeley: University of California Press, 1967) pp. 103-104, 132-134.

were organised and were severely repressed by the British government, especially in Punjab because of the violence which broke out during the demonstrations. The Punjab repression and the Khilafat grievances somehow became linked as two compelling reasons for both Hindus and Muslim to join hands and oppose the government.[197]

It seemed that Hindu-Muslim entente had come into existence. Demonstrations against the government showed a new technique leaders could use with some success. This led to the two new political bodies:

1. The All-India Khilafat Committee, and

2. The *Jamiat-al-'ulama-al-Hind*

Although both these bodies were Muslim, Gandhi saw a tremendous potential in the All-India Khilafat Committee to unite Hindus and Muslims against the common enemy, the British rule. He enlisted his support on the Khilafat issue and this brought about a degree of Hindu-Muslim unity. For many Muslims and Hindus, this was a dream come true because in the past both these communities had tried some kind of rapprochement.[198] These efforts were undertaken by a group of barristers who were devoted to the principle of self-determination and who were capable enough to

---

[197]   Minault, p. 66.

[198]   Examples of these are the Allahabad conference of Hindu and Muslim leaders in 1910, the Lucknow Pact, the endorsement of self-government by the Muslim League in 1913 and also the fact that many Muslims had taken active part in the Indian National Congress right from its inception in 1880s. When Muslims formed their League, Muhammad Ali referred to the League not in opposition to the Indian National Congress but rather saying that both were akin to two different trees on each side of the same road whose branches met.

constitutionally negotiate to safeguard Muslim rights.[199] On the other hand, the *Jamiat-al-Ulama-al-Hind* as an organisation led by religious scholars who favoured religious appeals and used emotional tones. Also, they favoured journalism in place of constitutional debates. Gandhi's style was different from both of these. It was taking the case to the public, in their very place of work whether to a street sweeper or a small *dukan walla* (shopkeeper) or in to workers in the factories. Although the styles of approaching problem varied between leaders, the Indian mass as a whole found the concerns the leaders were raising very appealing.

The problem for both Hindu and Muslim leaders was inter-communal distrust. Gandhi decided to meet with Muslim leaders in order to forge a plan whereby Hindus and Muslims could live in harmony. Muslim leaders, and among them Abdul Bari in particular, were quite anxious to meet Gandhi in order to get support from him so that the Ali brothers, who were interned, could be released. Abdul Bari met Gandhi in 1918.[200] During the meeting, Gandhi explained to Abdul Bari the potential he saw if Muslims and Hindus united to achieve their common goal of *swarajya* (self-government). Gandhi made his intention perfectly clear for joining hands with Muslims in a show of solidarity. For him it was the attainment of *swarajya*. Gandhi agreed to support Abdul Bari in getting a release for the Ali brothers. He wrote a letter to the Viceroy of India to request the release of the Ali brothers. In a letter he wrote to Muhammad Ali he said,

> ". . . My interest in your release is quite selfish. We have a common goal and I want to utilize your services

---

[199] Minault, p. 67.

[200] Minault quoting from Muhammad Inayatullah, *Hasrat al afaq ba I'afat-e-Majmua al-Akhlaq* (short biography of Abdul Bari), (Lucknow: Firangi Mahal, 1929), pp. 22-23.

to the uttermost, in order to achieve the goal . . . the realisation of Swarajya.[201]

With the agreement with Muslims secured, Gandhi must have felt very strong. He could now implement many of the tactics he had already used in South Africa. Gandhi found an opportunity for such with the passing of the Rowlatt Bills on March 18, 1919. There was a widespread opposition to this legislation. Hindus and Muslims held several meetings to protest the Bills, but to no avail. The Rowlatt Bills introduced wartime measures in time of peace. The Bills would give powers to the Police to search people and arrest them and throw them in jails without trial. Those that were thrown into jails would have no right to appeal. New taxation would be imposed. When Gandhi saw there was widespread and almost unanimous opposition to this Bill, he declared *satyagraha* (struggle for the truth).[202] Gandhi took a promise from his followers that they would disobey the Rowlatt Bill but remain totally non-violent. [203] Abdul Bari agreed to this, although he claimed that the British government passed this Bill at the time only to keep Muslims from protesting decisions of the Peace Conference that would decide the fate of the Ottoman empire. Abdul Bari was not alone in this kind of thinking. Most Muslims were convinced the Rowlatt Bills were unnecessary and designed only to keep Muslims from protesting the upcoming Peace Conference.

---

[201] Minault, p. 68. See also" The Emergence of Ulema in the Politics of India and Pakistan..." in http://www.scribd.com/doc/100495764/ The-Emergence-of-Ulema-in-the-Politics-of-India-and-Pakistan-1918-1949.

[202] Gandhi had used this technique successfully in South Africa. This was a philosophy he believed in which the oppressor would be opposed without any violence. If he is punished, he would endure it without retaliating or using any form of violence until the oppressor begins to see the satya (truth) himself and retreats.

[203] see Satyagraha-*Meaning and Efficacy in The Rise and Growth of Congress in India (1885-1920),* pp. 185-186.

The Ali brothers accepted *satyagraha* and they also agreed to another request from Gandhi—to write a letter to the Viceroy refusing to abide with the terms proposed in the internment. This may not have been the best thing to do, though, because of the government's sensitivity at the time. The British government already considered the Ali brothers as the agitators in the Khilafat issue. They had also refused to sign any pledges to the government that they would stop their activities regarding the Khilafat agitation. When the government received their letter opposing the Rowlatt Bills they were thrown into jail.[204] The *satyagraha* began with Gandhi's request for a *hartal* (general strike) on March 30. In a very interesting report cited in Sir Reginald Craddock's *The Dilemma in India*, we are told that the *Hartal* was very carefully organised by Gandhi. It coincided with the visit of the Prince of Wales and while the prince was not directly insulted, the effects of *hartal* could be felt everywhere. This led to embarrassing moments for a new Viceroy, Reading, who had just taken over from his predecessor, retired Viceroy Chelmsford[205] Later, because the preparation was not complete and because the leaders wanted this strike to be really widespread, its date was changed to April 6th. Followers in Delhi, however, ignored the call and proceeded to strike. There was violence. Police arrived and opened fire, killing several people. This stunned people. Next day, Hindus and Muslims held meetings in which both embraced each other and vowed to remain united. There were shouts of "Hindu Muslim bhay bhay (Hindus and Muslims are brothers, brothers). Memorial services were held at the Jama Masjid, the main mosque in Delhi. It is interesting to note that the climate favouring amity between Hindus and Muslims had become so

---

[204] Gandhi was not too pleased with the way things went. Gandh wanted total non-violence in his Satyagraha principle but he felt the letter Ali brothers wrote to the Viceroy contained inflammatory words. *See Collected Works of Gandhi,* 15:290. See also *Nuqush,* 2, pp. 61-65; 152.

[205] See Reginald Craddock, *Dilemma in India* (London: Constable & CO. Ltd. 1929) pp. 194-196

strong that even the most staunch Hindu, Swami Shradhanand, attended the memorial service in the mosque.[206]

The agitation against the Rowlatt Act was so severe and so widespread that it brought about another very sad incident in Jalianwalla Bag, Amritsar, on April 13, 1919. This was the incident when General O'Dwyer of the British Police gunned down 378 demonstrators as they were peacefully demonstrating at Jalianwalla Bag.[207] In 1920, when the British government produced the Hunter Commission's report into the Jalianwalla Bag incident, this became a national issue. The *satyagraha* had a potential to unite all Indians under one cause for the very first time. This seemed to be coming to pass. True, there were some violent skirmishes reported here and there, but these were not inter-communal. Rather, these were between the demonstrators and the police. This suggested that the police were using very highhanded methods to put down demonstrations. Reports tell us[208] it was quite a sight to see Hindu-Muslim fraternising and Hindus readily admitted to the Muslim Mosques and Muslims into the Hindu temples. There were cries of "Hindu Musalman ki jai" (victory to Hindu-Muslim unity) and even *"Hindu Musalman ki jai ho!* (may there be victory for Hindu-Muslim unity).

In a very interesting poem I discovered in the Proscribed Material, we read the deep feelings with which Hindus and Muslims had become united. The poet Jadulal Narandas composed the following lines:

---

[206] See G. R. Thursby, Hindu Muslim Relations in British India (Leiden: Brill, 1975).

[207] Craddock, *Dilemma in India* (London: Constable & Co. Ltd. 1929) pp. 194-196. See also Minault quoting from *Congress Punjab Inquiry Report.* (1919, 19201, and also Parliamentary Papers 1920, vol. XIV, cmnd 687.

[208] Minault quoting from *Independent,* October 12, 1919. See p. 232 in Minault.

Hindus and Muslims united into one; say Victory, O Hindustan!
This our land, our country; give your life for it
We are brothers in a family, children of Mother India
Hindus, Parsis, Muslims all say: Victory, O Victory, Hindustan!
Temple and Masjid are both spheres of the Most High
There should be no difference between brother and brother
With one-ness and being one, let us create the unity
Let *satyagraha* flow in our veins; say Victory, O Hindustan!
Dham, dham, dham, dham! let the flags flutter high
Ring the bells of swarajya and say; Victory, O Hindustan!
Our souls are higher than swords and guns and spears
Bodies fall dead but our souls are eternal; say Victory, O Hindustan!
Angels of Paradise anxiously await you with a garland of Victory
Give your life in the valley of Motherland; say Victory, O Hindustan!

Hindu Muslim ek thai ne jay jay bolo Hindustan
Aa bhumi aapni desh aapno e par jan karo kurban
Ek kutunbi bhay aaapne maata Bharat na santaan
Hindu Parsi Muslim sau Jay Jay bolo Hindustan
Mandir ane Masjid banne che ishwar kera uncha dhaam
Bhay-Bhay maan bhed na hoi Jay Jay bolo Hindustan
Ek nek-ne ek tek-thi karo ekta kerun paan
rag rag maan satyagrah redi Jay Jay bolo Hindustan
Dham dham dham dham dhara dhrujavo farkavo uncha nishan
Swara jya danka gagdavi Jay Jay bolo Hindustan
Talwaro banduk bhala-thi uncha che atma na sthaan
Sharir padde pan e to ammar Jay Jay bolo Hindustan
Vijay maar lai Swarga-Sundari tatpar che kawa sanmaan
Matru-vedi maan pran arpine Jay Jay bolo Hindustan[209]

Unfortunately, this unity dampened somewhat because of two incidents. First, Gandhi was upset that not all demonstrations were non-violent. Violence had occurred, and therefore he felt obliged to call off his civil-disobedience

---

[209] See Jadulal Narandas, Say "Victory O Victory Hindustan" in Publications Proscribed by the Government of India (London, 1985), entry number 396.

campaign. Gandhi blamed himself for what he called the "Himalayan miscalculation" he had made, his failiure to realise that his people needed more practice on how to conduct a peaceful demonstration. Muslims did not like this and felt that Gandhi and his followers were backing down. Also, strict Muslims and Hindus were questioning whether it was right to use mosques and temples for political reasons.

Another reason that affected Hindu-Muslim unity was the third Anglo-Afghan war of May and June 1919. In this war, Amanullah of Afghanistan attacked India, saying that the unrest in India against the British government was also affecting Afghanistan. He said the British were unjust and he was attacking British outposts across his border in sympathy for his Indian brothers, both Hindus as well as Muslims. Somehow, Hindus were not convinced by this explanation. The idea that an Afghan ruler could invade India through the "Khyber Pass to link up with the frontier Muslims excited the primordial fears of the Hindu plainsmen.[210]

It is to be noted that these agitations were not as hollow as one particular source suggests.[211] Bamford seems to think that these agitations were precipitated for only one reason—"they succumbed to economic condition. When crops during the years 1922 and 1923 improved, financial stability returned and the agitations totally failed.[212] This statement makes little sense given that no leader in their speeches ever seemed to mention or raise the issue in the Khilafat movement. On the contrary, Muslims showed they were more generous as they contributed to the Khilaf at fund.

The reason why All-India Khilafat Committee was formed was not to address economic or social conditions. As we have

---

[210] See Minault, pp. 71-72.
[211] C. Bamford, *Histories Khilafat Movements* (Delhi, 1925), the Non-Co-operation, pp. 10ff
[212] Ibid., p. 13.

already seen earlier, Muslims had become suspicious, especially during the Balkan wars, that the British empire was conniving with other European powers to get rid of the Ottoman empire. When the First World War opened, Muslims wholeheartedly supported the British government. They were prepared to give the British government benefit of doubt only because of the solemn pledge the government gave the Indian Muslims.

The Khilafat agitation began only when Muslims clearly saw that the pledges given were not worth the paper they were written on. Then it was that the All-India Khilafat Committee on came into existence. The reason was simple—to use all possible means to make the British government understand Indian Muslims' attachment to the office of the Caliphate.

It is worth asking why the Khilafat Committee did not use the Muslim League for their movement. After all, the Muslim League already existed as a body recognised even by the government. The answer could perhaps be that the Khilafat leaders felt a need for a totally fresh outlook in an organisation that had no history or any other agenda except to address the problem of the Caliphate. In this regard, this was more of a religious issue and would be better dealt with as such by the Khilafat Committee. Thus we find that the speeches of the Khilafat leaders had religious tones. Also when the leaders met with officials to present their grievances, they always appealed in religious stones. When a Khilafat deputation addressed the Viceroy in 1920 it appealed that if the British government would meet their demands, the world would be safe for democracy.[213]

In any case, the Muslim League was not a fully functioning body and several of their meetings had to be adjourned because of the members' apathy. Many meetings had to be cancelled simply because of the lack of a quorum. The League had sent a deputation to the Paris Peace Conference but failed

---

[213] see A.C. Niemeijer, *The Khilafat Movement in India 1919-1924*, p. 70.

to impress the British government.[214] What was required, therefore, was not only a functioning body but a body without any previous history of loyalty to the British government. Another apparent consideration was that the body should be entirely religious to represent the interests of Muslims and to address the grievances they had against the British government.

The new movement held their first meeting in Bombay on March 20, 1919, attended by fifteen thousand Muslims from Bombay. It was in this meeting that the Khilafat Committee was formed.

It is noteworthy that the Shi'a *'ulama* showed anxieties equal to their Sunni brethren. Commenting on this, Shaikh Mushir Husain of Kidwai of Gadia (also known as al-Qidwai) observed this phenomenon as a proof of revival of Islamic spirit which "dominates the sentiments of racial nationalism or even patriotism is demonstrated by Ayatollahs in Iran that even they, although being Shi'as, have accepted and stand shoulder to shoulder with the rest of the Muslims in accepting the Ottoman Sultan as the chief head of the Muslim nation".[215]

In the meeting it was resolved to:

1. have an Indian Muslim representation in the Peace Conference.

2. ask the Government that Constantinople remain part of the Ottoman empire.

3. select an all-Indian Muslim deputation should be recommended to see the viceroy.[216]

---

[214] Minault, pp. 72-73.

[215] Shaikh Mushir Husain Kidwai of Gadia: "Islam and Nationalism" in *Muslim Review*, 1919, pp. 249-253.

[216] Minault quoting from *The Independent*, March 26, 1919.

The above resolutions passed by the Bombay Khilafat Committee did not run parallel to resolutions Abdul Bari and the Ali brothers gave Gandhi when he launched his *satyagraha*. It will be remembered Abdul Bari and the Ali brothers had agreed on petitions and non-violent tactics. In the Bombay Khilafat Committee, while some favoured petitions, others clearly felt that petitions were no help at all. They felt that what was required was not just a body of intellectual Khilafat leaders but a vast, organised Muslim united front on the question of the Caliphate, so that it could become a mobilised movement. At just about the same time the Viceroy sent a reply to the earlier request Indian Muslims had made for a deputation to meet with him. In the reply the Viceroy declined to meet with Muslims because he said the British government already knew what the Muslim demands were and therefore it would serve no purpose to meet with him.[217]

On July 5 1919, when the Bombay Khilafat Committee met again this idea of a broader-based, mass movement was widely favoured instead of passive petitions. In this meeting it was resolved to:

1. start branches of the Khilafat movement all over India.

2. hold frequent meetings, and to keep Muslims all over India fully aware of the issues.

3. translate Muslim feeling of frustration into effective pressure on the government.

By doing this, it was hoped, the British government could be brought to understand two major Muslim demands:

1. the continuation of the office of the Caliphate in Constantinople under the Ottoman Sultan, and

---

[217] Minault, p. 73.

2. ensuring continuation of his suzerainty over the Islamic holy places.

In the Muslim Review 1919, al-Qidwai wrote to say that Muslims must be ruled by a Muslim. Al-Qidwai quoted, in support of his argument, a verse from the Qur'an (4 :59)[218]

The Muslim League drew up a special appeal to all Muslims in India[219] for an All-India Muslim Conference in which there would be representatives from all groups and all regions in India. The purpose would be to draw up a universal programme of action that would be followed by all Muslims in India. The proposal was drawn up and signed by recognised and respected members of the community. It was decided it would be held in Lucknow in September 1919.[220]

---

[218] "O ye who believe! Obey Allah and obey the Messenger and those charged with authority amongst you. (But) if you differ in anything among yourselves, (then) refer it to Allah and His Messenger, if you do believe in Allah and the Last Day: That is best, and most suitable for final determination." Al-Qidwai, referring to this verse in the Qur'an, said that the ruler should be among Muslims themselves, for otherwise there would be no harmony between the commands of Allah, the commands of the prophet and the laws of the king or the president. Just as by "the Prophet" was meant the Prophet Muhammad, so by the phrase in the verse quoted, "those among you" meant "those among Muslims" pp. 251-252.

[219] The Muslim League expected wide support from all Muslims including Shi`as.

[220] This proposal was signed by respectable members like Hon. Sir Ibrahim H. Khan Jaffer, Sayyid Zabur Ahmed, Nawab Sir Zulfiqar Ali Khan, Sir Fazlibhai Currimbhai, Bombay; Seth Haji Abdullah Harun, Karachi ; Fazl al-Haqq, Calcutta; Dr. Mumtar Ahmad Ansari and H.A. Khan, Delhi. Also a signatory was Sayyid Raza Ali, who was a Shi`a and was also an Uttar Pradesh Barrister.

When the All-India Muslim Conference took place in September, it was a very successful meeting.[221] Muslims became mobilised. It was proposed that October 17th. 1919 would be observed by all Muslims in India as the All-India Khilafat Day. This would be a day of an all-out strike all across India. It would be a day for prayers, fasting, *hartal*, and public meetings. Muslim leaders appealed for support from Hindus as well. All over India Sunni Muslims strictly observed this. It was supported also by Shi`as. Most importantly, even Gandhi addressed the meeting. October 17, 1919, was observed even in remote parts of India.

The leaders were astounded at this success. It was realized that this momentum should be organised at a national level, It was necessary to keep it going before it became forgotten. An all-India conference was therefore called to meet in Delhi on November 23-24, 1919, when a complete plan of activities would be decided upon.

In the November conference, the *'ulama* who were in Delhi at the time for the opening of the *Jamiat-al-'ulama-al-Hind* were heavily represented. More than half of three hundred or so delegates were from Uttar Pradesh alone.

At this meeting four important resolutions were passed. These were:

1. Muslims were to boycott the peace celebrations planned by the British government for December (unless the British government decided to accord the Ottoman empire a just settlement regarding the Caliph).

---

[221] There were minor squabbles at the beginning of the meeting over details such as who would preside. Once this was resolved, the meeting was under way supported by all Indians, Muslims as well as Hindus.

2. Muslims had a religious duty to withdraw cooperation from the British government if the Caliphate became jeopardised by the Peace settlement.

3. If Turkish peace proposals were unjust, Muslims were to institute a progressive boycott of European goods.[222]

4. The Khilafat Conference was to appoint a delegate who would go to England and represent Muslims' cause to the Home government.[223]

Perhaps the most important breakthrough came the following day, on 24th November 1919. At a highly publicised joint Hindu-Muslim conference, Gandhi declared Hindus were uniting with Muslims on their grievance over the Caliphate. Even Pundit Jawaharlal Nehru, Swami Shradhanand and Pundit Malaviya were present. The reason Gandhi gave for uniting with Muslims was that Muslims were demanding what was a just cause[224]

By the end of 1919, the Khilafat Committee set up organisations and adopted methods for demonstrating and propagating the Caliphate cause.

---

[222] This proposal was not fuJly endorsed by Gandhi and merchants because it would hit the economy and their businesses, but it passed, anyway.

[223] This group included Maulana Abdul Bari, Dr. Mukhtar Ahmad Ansari, Raja of Mahmudabad, Raza Ali, Pazul Haq, Sayyid Hussain and Seth Chotani.

[224] See Khaliquzzaman, p. 50. There were also interesting rumours that Gandhi had united with Muslims only as a gesture. Others insisted it was because Gandhi had struck a deal with Muslims that Muslims would stop slaughter of cows in return for Gandhits support. See Thursby, *Cow and Conflict in Hindu-Muslim Relations,* pp. 76-78.

The *'ulama* joined in, too, although they had founded their own organisation—the *Jamiat-al-'ulama-al-Hind* founded in 1919. This was to be a new political organisation. Its tactical approach was not different from that of the Khilafat Committee; except that they would present themselves as religious guides.

The *'ulama* thought of themselves as the upholders of the Shari'a and therefore they were the religious guides *par excellence*. In their view the upholding of the Caliphate was a religious issue. If they got involved in politics it was only because in it they saw the execution of their religious obligation. In order to fulfil their obligation collectively in a way in which all *'ulama* could take part they tried to organise an all-India association of *'ulama*.

Abdul Bari wrote to his friends in early 1919 that the problem of defending the Caliphate and the holy places was the issue in Shari'a and pointed to the need of organising a body of *'ulama* which could express unified opinions on Shari'a so that Muslims could be directed in their opinion.[225] Abdul Bari used this theme throughout his lectures everywhere. In support of this goal of his, he quoted the Qur'an and the *sira* (bioagraphy) of the Prophet. Abdul Bari seems to have known the problem that had plagued many Muslim organisations—disunity among the leaders and petty squabbles. He therefore urged the *'ulama* of different schools (Aligarh, Deoband, Bareilly, Badaun and Lucknow) to unite into one single body. He requested an all-India conference of ulama.

Abdul Bari also urged Sufis of all turuq (paths, plural of tariqa) to make united pronouncements on the question of the Caliphate. He urged them to mention in the Friday prayers and pray for the Caliph.

In displaying solidarity with Muslims of all walks of life, he also endeavoured to secure a unanimous *fatwa* which stated that:

---

[225] Abdul Bari Papers. Firangi Mahal, Lucknow.

1. the Caliph need not be a Qurayshite.

2. If anyone revolted against the Caliph, he would be put down even if he were himself a Qurayshite.

3. The holy places for Islam are defined to be all of Arabia. This would be the most sacred two places on earth for Muslims, Makkah and Madina. It would also include the city of Jerusalem in Palestine, the city of Najaf in Syria[226], and the city of Kerbala in Mesopotamia.[227]

The *fatwa* was not unanimously accepted.[228] The e *'ulama* discussed for themselves the general plan of action they would like to take. They also formed working committee.

---

[226] Najaf is important because of the tomb of Imam 'Ali ibn Abi Talib, the first Imam of the Shi`a Muslims. An important centre for Shi`a Muslims, Najaf has always been a symbol of Imam 'Ali's piety and his stand against the leaders he thought were autocratic and corrupt.

[227] Abdul Bari, *Ulama-e-Hind ka Fatwa Masala-e-Khilafat par.* Abdul Bari, a Sunni 'alim, put the cities of Najaf and Karbala in his *Fatwa* as the holy places for Muslims on earth to be included with Makka, Madina and Jerusalem. It is interesting because these two cities, Najaf and Karbala are the Shi`a centres of pilgrimage called the Ziyarat, next in importance to the obligatory Hajj pilgrimage all Muslims must perform in Makka, at least once in their lifetime, if they can. An important centre for the Shi`a Muslims, Karbala has always been a symbol for the fight against social injustices and unwanted domination by corrupt rulers. We shall see in later chapters that Karbala became an important paradigm for all Indian Muslims in their demand for a separate state after the collapse of the Khilafat movement.

[228] The *fatwa* was not unanimously accepted not because it included Najaf and Karbala as holy places. It was not accepted mainly because of internal rivalries among the 'ulama. Also, there were differences of opinion among the 'ulama as to whether such an approach would be useful.

In December 1919, the Congress, the Muslim League, the All-India Khilafat Committee and *Jamiat-al-'ulama-al-Hind* met simultaneously at Amritsar. The Ali brothers were released from prison in time for this conference. The Indian Congress meeting was presided over by Nehru; and it expressed complete solidarity with Muslims in their Caliphate agitation. There was also an impromptu address, well received, by the just released from internment, Muhammad Ali.

The Muslim League did not do much business. Most of its productive time was spent on listening to talks by its members. The newly released Ali brothers had the podium most of the time. Nevertheless, it was clear that the Caliphate agitation was fully supported by all in the Congress as well.

The Khilafat Committee was presided over by Shaukat Ali. This was an impressive show, at the end of which the Khilafat Committee passed two main resolutions:

1. that if the British government agreed to peace terms against the tenets of Islam, they would be left with no choice but to defend their faith. The resolution did not specify how would they defend their faith in the event the Peace terms went against the tenets of Islam.[229]

2. that they should send a delegation to England and also to Constantinople to express solidarity with the Caliph.

During the meeting, several measures were discussed to build up the Khilafat organisation. In order to start their measures, they would require funds. It was resolved to start

---

[229] Minault seems to think that this was in response to pressures the Khilafat Committee had from the Bombay faction. There was no mention of the economic boycott or the noncooperation movement because these were already resolved upon in November of the same year. See Minault, p. 83.

with a fund of a million Rupees. These monies would be collected by means of donations.

It was also resolved to circulate the drafted constitution to all districts and provinces throughout India. These districts and provinces would hold their meetings and approve them.

There was always one way the government officials could be approached. It was by means of a group representing the community taking with it a petition to be handed to an official. During several Khilafat meetings in 1919 another approach being discussed was non-violent demonstrations or *hartal*; and if these two methods did not work, then non-cooperation with the government. While most in the Khilafat meetings and conferences supported the new approach, the Ali brothers decided to still use the traditional approach, by way of deputations. Two such deputations were planned; the f i r s t was to seek Viceroy Chelmsford's approval for a delegation to visit England to present their case to the British government.

The deputation met with Viceroy Chelmsford on 19th January1920 and presented their plea for visiting England. They wanted to explain Muslim concern in the upcoming Paris Peace Conference which would decide the fate of the Ottoman empire. The deputation felt that the British policy makers were far removed from Indian Muslims not only from the point of distance

> but also in political and religious surroundings . . . (insisting) . . . on a settlement of such world-wide interest and importance as if it was solely . . . the concern of the small fraction of His Majesty's subjects of British birth and Christian faith. From (us) they expect . . . willing submission, to the dictates of their narrowly conceived and far from Imperial statesmanship[230]

---

[230] K. K. Aziz, *The Khilafat Movement 1915-1933: A Documentary Record*, pp. 65-66.

They told the Viceroy that the preservation of the Caliphate, as a temporal no less than a spiritual institution, is the very essence thereof; and nothing can change it, alter it or dismember it.[231] They reminded the Viceroy of the British government's pledges at the beginning of the war regarding the possessions of the Ottoman empire and the sanctity of the holy places in the Jazirat al-'Arab (all Arab lands in the peninsula of Arabia). In demanding this, they were concerned also with their 'eternal salvation' and they said this was the consideration on which no Muslim—including Ottoman Turks—could be made to acquiesce.[232]

In reply to the above, the Viceroy agreed to facilitate their voyage to England and tried to explain that the government would do all it could to place the feelings of Indian Muslims before the peace deliberations. The Viceroy requested Muslims to remain loyal to the British government, no matter what the outcome. The deputation refused to give any such assurance.[233]

The deputation led by Muhammad Ali arrived in England in February 1920. Within a few days, they met at the India Office with the deputy of Montague, H.A.L. Fisher. In this meeting, they reiterated their concerns. They also presented a new idea: that since the Ottoman Turks and Arabs had become enemies, there was a need to mediate between them and they felt that they should be allowed to mediate between these two groups of Muslims. They felt they had more right to mediate because this was a religious issue which should be left to Muslims to settle among thernselves.[234] The British government would not allow

---

[231] Ibid., p. 67.

[232] Ibid., p. 67.

[233] see Minault, p.87. Also see Aziz, pp. 77-78.

[234] In asking for this, I have no doubt, the delegation was anxious to fulfil an injunction in the Qur'an. See Sura 49:10 "When two parties among the believers quarrel with each other, make peace between them two. And if one of them transgresses (after the peace has been made between them) over the other, fight him all

such a request but even if it did, it is doubtful the Arabs of the Hejaz would have liked it. At this point, the Arabs welcomed the defeat of the Ottoman empire. They were rejoicing at the chance to create their own nationalistic homelands and seemed hardly to have been interested in any Islamic unity. It is said that if they were allowed to mediate between the Ottoman Turks and Arabs, there is no doubt that they (the Indian Muslims) would have enhanced their prestige in the eyes of the Muslim world. The Caliphate in the hands of the Ottomans would have survived in spite of the fact that the Ottoman empire itself was so weak, especially after the Balkan wars we mentioned in Chapter Two.

Another thing the deputation did in London was to emphasise that their mission in all this was not political. They emphasized and impressed upon the British government as well as the British public that their mission was purely religious. In this, they emphasised that they were duty bound to take up the cause of the Caliphate as t h e i r own cause because they said the Caliph was the defender of their faith:

> Islam is supernational and not national, that the basis of Islamic sympathy is not a conunon domicile or common parentage, but a common outlook on life and common culture . . . the embodiment of that common culture is Khilafat. Islam is . . . a complete scheme of life . . . it has two centres. The personal centre is the Khalifa and the local centre is the island of Arabia, the Sanctuary of Islam, the land of the Prophets . . . The Khalifa is something more than a Pope and cannot be 'Vaticanised.' But he is also less than

---

of you together until he accepts Allah's injunction. If he does, make peace between them and deal with full justice and be fair; for Allah loves those who are just. Verily the believers are one brotherhood. Therefore make peace between your brother and be conscious of Allah so that you may receive His Mercy".

a Pope, for he is not infallible . . . His chief function has always been defence of our faith . . . [235]

In their meeting with Prime Minister Lloyd George himself, they were not able to convince him of anything. After hearing what the Muslim delegate had to say, Lloyd George wondered why the Indian Muslims be against Arab independence when it was the Arabs who had proclaimed it themselves. Muhammad Ali replied to this question simply by saying that if given the opportunity to make peace between the two quarrelling Muslim brethren, the Amir Faisal would see, as a Muslim himself, that the Arabs could have what they wanted and still be under the Ottoman empire.[236]

Further, the Indian Muslim delegation reminded Lloyd George also about the pledge he had given to the Indian Muslims regarding Constantinople, Thrace, Asia Minor and areas which were inhabited by a Muslim majority: that these would remain under the Ottoman empire.

After having heard the delegation, Lloyd George used to the optimum his language of diplomacy and explained to the delegation how Britain considered itself as the largest Muslim empire in the world. Therefore, he wanted the delegation to know that Turkey would not be treated any different than the other two Christian countries (he meant Germany and Austria) which went to war against Britain. The fate of these two Christian countries was that they were dealt with ruthlessly and their possessions taken away from them. Austria was an empire but

"what is she now? She has fallen to her fragments are scattered about . . . [and] . . . What has happened in Germany? We have taken Alsace-Lorraine away from Germany. The whole of Poland has been taken away from

---

[235] Muhammad Ali, *Selected Writings and Speeches*, 2 :1 9ff.
[236] See Aziz, pp. 22 ff.

her, and we have imposed upon her very stern and severe terms[237].

And so he said that he did not want any Muslim in India to think that this war was a crusade against slam.[238] Turkey, therefore, he said is not being treated severely because it is Muslim, but the principles of self-determination would have to be applied.

This reply must have sunk the hearts of the Indian Muslim delegates. In the month of May 1920, when the terms of the Treaty of Sevres were released, it was all that the Indian Muslims had been afraid of. The Arab countries were to become independent of the Ottoman empire. Syria, Palestine, and Mesopotamia were put under French and British mandates. Eastern Thrace and Smyrna were given to Greece. The Dodecanese Islands went to Italy. Constantinople remained with the Turks, although their Straits were internationalised. The Ottoman empire signed the Treaty on August 20, 1920[239]. This was the end of the Ottoman empire.

When the Government of India issued its communique on Turkish peace terms for the consumption of Indian Muslims

---

[237] K.K. Aziz, *The Indian Khilafat Movement 1915-1933: A Documentary Record,* pp. 110-111.

[238] It appears very strange that he said this because it was the same Prime Minister, Lloyd George, who had said not so long previously when proposing gratuity to General Allenby these words : "The name of General Allenby will be ever renowned as that of the brilliant commander who fought and won the last and most triumphant of the Crusades. It was his good fortune, by his skill, to bring to a glorious end an enterprise which absorbed the chivalry of Europe for centuries. *We forget now that the military strength of Europe was concentrated for generations upon this purpose* in vain, and a British Army under the command of General Allenby achieved it and achieved it finally. (italics are mine). See K.K. Aziz, p. 110.

[239] See Minault, p. 90.

it listed sixteen points stating the reasons why such a treaty was favoured by the British government. It is instructive to read because of its views on the Caliphate and other issues. On the Caliphate, the Communique mentioned that this issue is for Muslims only to decide. However, the Communique reads, Muslims cannot acquiesce in the statement that the Caliphate of the Ottoman Sultan remained unchanged in its temporal attributes for the last thirteen centuries or that it implied any temporal allegiance on part of Indian Muslims. The Communique said these were only propositions because the temporal power of the Caliphate had gone through

> the most violent fluctuations during the last thirteen centuries . . . reduced to nothing for over two centuries when the Khalifa (Caliph) was the mere spiritual head of Islam under the Mameluk dynasty of Egypt.[240]

With the Treaty published, the Khilafat delegation returned home to advance the Khilafat cause even further. This was to demand from the British government self-government. As a matter of fact, while the delegate was in Europe, the Khilafat Committee at home was already debating on new methods to promote its cause. It considered Gandhi's method of non-cooperation with the British government. When the delegate returned home from England, Muhammad Ali proclaimed in his speech that the Caliphate cause could become a reality only when India was in the hands of Indians themselves. Therefore, self-government was the only answer. The means and method to achieve this would be noncooperation with the British government.

In doing so, Muhammad Ali was also assuring Hindus that aspirations Muslims had for *swarajya* were not any different theirs. Muhammad Ali always maintained that just as Indian Muslims cannot get away from their being Muslims, so too they

---

[240] Aziz quoting from *The Indian Annual Register 1921*, Part I, pp. 185-192.

cannot get away from their being Indians. Both, their being Indian and their being Muslim, always went together. In his pronouncement for self-government, Muhamad Ali was using the Caliphate as a symbol for freedom, social freedom as well as political. Self-government became a sacred cause, and the new method to achieve this, non-cooperation, became a religious obligation.[241] This was a turning point in the history of Indian Muslims because this sense of symbolism and a sense of sacred cause, it can be argued, eventually turned Muslims to demand for their own Muslim land they would call Pakistan.

In this regard, the year 1920 was very significant for arousing Indian Muslims. Several pro-Khilafat and anti-British publications began to appear. These were considered seditious by the British government and were proscribed. In one such publications, we come across a poem composed by Muhammad Ali himself. Muhammad Ali calls it "Songs of the Free Birds"(*Bulbulan-i-Hurriyat keh Taraaneh*). In this poem, Muhammad Ali indicates strong bonds Indian Muslims have with Turks, not only because they are the bearers of the seat of the Caliphate but also because their garrisons were protecting the two holy places of Islam, Makkah and Madina (*Haramayn Sharif*). The Turks therefore warranted all the support they could get in retaining their Ottoman territories and preserving the Caliphate.

'O Allah! protect the honour of my Turkish warriors
They protect the gates of the most holiest Tomb of the Prophet
Enemies in milllions want to destroy the Ka'ba
O Allah! protect everything and everyone in the Ka'ba
The great arrogance and the great indifference
Shown by Europe has no limit no bounds
O Allah! bring down Your curse upon them
O Allah! give the Turkish swords that fine cut
To remind others of its earlier conquests
Ilahi ! aabru rakhna meray Turkie jawanon ki

---

[241] See Minault, p. 91.

Diyar-i Mustafa khayr-ul-wala keh paasbanon ki
Gulistaan-i Harm keh tak mein sayyao
Ilahi! hay lakhon khayr-i murghan harm keh aashyanon ki
Ghurur-o kubar-o nakhwat hadd seh guzra ahle-i Europe ka
Ilahi ! daalna un peh bal aaen aasmanon ki
Ilahi ! teghe Turkie ko woh-i jauhar ata kar deh
keh as jaay-i har ek ko yaad agli daastanon ki[242]

In another poem, we found a poet praising the mother of Muhammad Ali for inspiring Muhammad Ali to do everything, even if it meant to die in the cause of the Khilafat:

"0 My Son Give Your Life for the Khilafat
So said Muhammad Ali's mother,
0 my son, give your life for Khilafat,
You will gain good of both the worlds
As your name will be included
Among the martyrs for Khilafat
Oh Muhammad Ali and Shaukat
Sacrifice your lives in the cause of Khilafat
Jaan Beta Khilafat pe De Do
Boli amma Muhammad Ali ki, jaan beta Khilfat pe de do
Din-0-Dunya men paaoge 'izza t naam hoga Shahid-khilafa t
Ay Muhammad Ali aur Shaukat, jaan beta khilafat pe de do"[243]

Muslim leaders in 1920 began to combine their own forces. Three important activities took place in this year showing one clear purpose. This purpose was to use the Khilafat symbolism to arouse Muslims so that they would aspire for their own *Dar al-Islam*. These three activities were, firstly, the *'ulama* began in earnest the Khilafat propaganda in the villages of Uttar Pradesh and Sind. Secondly, Maulana Mahmud al-Hasan, who was interned in Malta because the British government had

---

[242] MaulanaM uhammad Ali, *Bulbulan-i Hurriyat keh Taraaneh*, Proscribed Material, Entry number 1426. See appendix 2.

[243] See Shaikh Anvar Ahmad, *Ah-i Mazluman*, Proscribed Material, Entry number 1392. See Appendix 3.

considered him an activist1 was released in 1920. Maulana Mahmud al-Hasan became influential in enrolling the Deobandis into the Khilafat movement, and thirdly, it was in this year that some '*ulama* gave a *fatwa* to perform *hijrat* to neighbouring Afghanistan. While the political leaders were engaged in discussions and meetings regarding the implementation of the non-cooperation programme, Muslim religious leaders were gathering their own forces. They were steadily gathering momentum going into the villages in Sind and in Uttar Pradesh propagating Khilafat agitation. The greatest help they received in this regard was the release of Maulana Mahmud al-Hasan from his long internment on Malta. Mahmud al-Hasan was well received at the Bombay port by well recognized leaders who included among others personalities like Abdul Bari, Gandhi, Shaukat Ali, Hafiz Mahmud Ahmad and Kafayatullah. In the days that followed Mahmud al-Hasan travelled extensively convincing the Deobandi '*ulama* to join the Khilaf at movement. With the Deobandi '*ulama* joined in, they focused on the shrines of pirs in Sind and in Uttar Pradesh. There were in Sind a number of pirs[244] who were involved with *the Anjuman-i-Khuddam-i-Kaaba* saw earlier. These pirs also readily joined the Khilafat movement. With '*ulama* joining the Khilafat movement, the masses followed too.[245]

---

[244] *Pirs* are Sufi saints. Earlietpirs had converted the Sindh to Islam. When they died, their burial places became shrines controlled by their lineal descendants. The shrines were important centres for Muslims to meet not only for worship but also as protest centres. The shrines were also used by the *Mujahidin* for their activity against the British government. Moreover, their importance was also derived from the fact that they controlled large landholdings. See Minault, p. 105.

[245] In one entry of the Proscribed Material, we found a booklet containing a question and answer session Mahmud al-Hasan gave to the public. Mahmud al-Hasan, as we know, was one of the highly respected '*ulama* and a leader of the Deoband seminary. His opinions carried great weight among the masses. In one public meeting, someone asked him: Is it necessary, from the point of

view of Islam, to join the Khilafat movement, Non-co-operation movement and freedom movements or not? If it is necessary for Muslims to join in these movements, what is the status of a Muslim who opposes this act? *Tark-i mawalat-o Swaraj mein shirkat zaruri hay ya na jaiz? Agar zaruri hay to jo shakhs iskay khilaf ho wuh kaisa hay?* Mahmud al-Hasan replied: You gentlemen are no doubt aware of the fact that the enemies of Allah have dishonoured, to the greatest extent, the Ka'ba, the final resting place of the Messenger of Allah Sallallahu 'alayhi wa Sallama (May Allah send peace upon him), Syria, Jerusalem, Taif, Baghdad, Karbala, Palestine, Egypt, Basra etc., etc.,. In my own presence, all these sacred places were subjected to extremely repressive measures. The protectors of the Ka'ba were humiliated to the extreme. The Ottoman empire was dismantled with dirty tricks and treachery. Muslims on the whole were treated similarly at other places. In view of all this, is there a single Muslim anywhere who would want to keep still and quiet? Therefore, these are the reasons why the Muslims of India supported non-cooperation, in order to perform acts made incumbent by Allah. Thus, in my opinion, the present movement is excellent and to join it is absolutely incumbent upon each and every Muslim. Any opposition to it would tantamount to opposing Islam and that would amount to a great sin. *Aap haazaraat is marsei nawaaqif nah hongay ke Khuda ka dushmanon ne harm-i Muharram aur Aramgah Rasul Allah Sallallahu 'Alayhi wa Sallama, Sham, Baytul Muqaddas, Tazf, Baghdad, Karbala, F i l i s t i n e, Misr, Basra waghayra waghayra ki kis qadar be hurmati ki. Khud bandeh ki maujudgi in muqadda maqaqmaat par kiya kiya ghazab dhai gayi. Muhafazeen-i Haramayn ki kis darje be in tihaai tauhin-o tazleel ki. Sal tanat-i Usmaniya ko makari ghaddari se tukray karwa diya. Aur Musalmanon ke saath dusri jageh kiya kiya muzalim kiya. In sab baton ko sun kar kaun kambakht Musalman hoga keh jo khamosh rahay. Pas yehi wajheh hay Hindustan ke Musalmanon na is Khuda ke Faraz-i azam keh ada karne ko aur mukhalafeen ke qattai defah ko tark-i rnawalat-i un-i Nasar jhoroo kiya. Pas Bandeh ke nazdik mawjooda tehrik bahut acchha-I hai a u r is me shirkat har Muslman ko faraaz-i 'din hai. Jo is ke khilaf hai wuh Islam ke saath sakht dushmani karta hai, jo keh*

It is to be noted that the pirs preached in Khilafat meetings all over Sind a message that would clearly instigate Muslims into thinking about a land that would truly be *Dar al-Islam*. They said unequivocally that the British government and their alliance of European powers (they referred to them as infidels) had taken over the holy cities of Islam. It was therefore important for Muslims not to cooperate with the British government. If they did, the message from the *'ulama* was that they would be condemned in the Hereafter into *Jahannum* (Hellfire).

As a result of this, at the February 1920 provincial Khilafat meeting, when the *pirs* spoke from the podium that was shared by Abdul Bari and Shaukat Ali, some of them called for the necessity of Muslims to attain their own political power since Islam could never flourish under the subjugation of the non-Muslims.[246] Among several publications that appeared at this time and were proscribed were the ones that were mobilising the masses by invoking the Karbala event.[247] In a collection bearing a title "Crying for India' a Successful (*g i r y a Hind-i Najat*) we found:

---

ek Gunah-i 'azim hay. See Mahmud al-Hasan, Mahud-ul-Hasan Maulana, Proscribed Material, Entry number 1518, Qaurni Press, Deoband, 1920. It is significant to note that this material was published in Deoband and this time the tract also gives the name of the Press in Deoband.

[246] Minault, p. 105.

[247] We shall have quite a bit more to say about the importance of Karbala's `Ashura tragedy in the next chapter. It is significant to note here that Karbala's `Ashura tragedy in early 1920's was used by Indian Muslims to arouse the anti-British feelings. Later, as the Khilafat and non-cooperation movements collapsed and Muslims began to get concerned about the communal violence and their future as Muslims among the Hindu majority, Karbala's `Ashura tragedy was effectively used against Hindus in support of the separate Islamic state championed by the Muslim League, under Muhammad Ali Jinnah in his Pakistan movement.

You the Khilafat Committee, you are a jewel
You are the saviour of those who sacrifice their life
You have the protection of the Shah-i-Madina (The Prophet),
While I am now being put into prison
Why Hindus and Muslims are showing affection to each other
Why the alam[248] is the banner representing Khilafa[249]
There must be Allah's wise plans in this
While I am now being put into the prison
Those who choose to become the lovers of Khilafat
Will be blessed as they find place in heaven
I will break the law (for saying this)
Do not leave the Khilafat now
Listen this wahshi (this poet)
Turn never away from the Khilafat

---

[248] *alam* is an important symbol in Karbala. This was the flag that
'Abbas, the beloved brother of Imam al-Husayn, had carried. This
symbol arouses deep passion for Shi`a Muslims everywhere but
in the context of time when this poem was composed, this symbol
must have aroused deep passion not only for all Muslims but also
for Hindus. This was the time of Gandhi's non-coperation movement
in which Muslims and Hindus had united. We have in the proscribed
material several collections, some of them cited here where Hindus
and Muslims are referred to as *bhay-bhay*. Hindus were invited
and were responding to the invitation of Muslims to participate in
prayers. During Muharram processions, Hindus were joining all
Muslims. These poems carry the lament of the `*Ashura* tragedy
and the martyrdom of the family of The Prophet, including Imam
al-Husayn, and his six-month old son on the `*Ashura* day in Karbala.
Imam al-Husayn, before he left Madina to go to Kufa, he visited the
tomb of the Prophet. The poet is eluding to that incident here.

[249] Khilafat was the issue in Karbala as well. Muslims who called the
Imam al-Husayn to rise against Yazid had indicated in their letters
that the Caliphate of Islam really belonged to the rightful Imam
who was also the *Amir al-Mu'minin*. Interestingly, the *alam* raised
during the Abbasid revolution against the Umayyads in 750 C.E.
also rose up in the name of Karbala and used black flags to denote
their mourning for the Karbala event.

Haiy Khilafat Committee naagina
Jaan nisaron ka tu hay safina
Tera h a f i s hay shah-i Madina
Ham to jaatay hay ab Jail-khaanay
Kyun hay Hindu aur Muslim mein yeh ulfat
Kyun alam hay nishane-i khilafat
Hay Hhuda ki isme koi Hihat
Ham to jaatay hay ab Jail-khaanay
Jo banengay Khilafat kay jogey
Un par Allah ki Rehmat bogey
In ko firdaus mein ghar milengi
Ham to Qanun-shikani karengei
A& Khilfat ka daaman na choro
Dekho Wahshi na munh ab moro

The most important event that took place in the summer of 1920 was the *Hijrat* movement. One of the protests discussed at the Khilafat meetings was *hijrat,*[250] migration to the lands of Islam (*Dar al-Islam*). In Sind and in the North-West Frontier, this idea found some support. *Hijrat* was made duty for Muslims through the *fatwa* Abdul Bari issued with Maulana Abul Kalam Azad. Thousands of Muslims decided to leave their settled life in Sind and in the North-West Frontier to emigrate to nearby Afghanistan, considered by Muslims to be *Dar al-Islam*. This exodus to the 'promised land' was laden with hardships. First, the tribesmen raided the caravans of migrants, looting their personal belongings. Second, the excessive heat during the journey and lack of enough food and drinking water brought about disaster as many died of hunger and thirst. Third, when over 30,000 immigrants who survived the journey entered Afghanistan, the Amir of Afghanistan issued an order prohibiting further immigration to his country. Thousands of immigrants who had not yet entered had to return, destitute

---

[250] *Hijrat* is defined as a religious migration where a Muslim, in order to escape anti-Islamic persecution, or even to escape from the anti-shari'a system finds it necessary to emigrate to a land where he is able to freely practice Islam.

and disillusioned about their future. The Central Khilafat Committee issued a request asking Muslims not to despair but instead to join the non-cooperation alternative.[251]

The *Hijrat* movement failed to establish Indian Muslims en-masse in Afghganistan. But it showed the Khilafatist leaders the strength and the energy Muslims could display when sufficiently aroused. The Khilafatist leaders took the *'ulama* under their wings. Sub-committees were formed and were financed by the Central Khilafat Committee to tour the villages and speak about the Khilafat and non-cooperation. This proved very effective[252]. Gandhi toured throughout India with Shaukat Ali, urging support from the mass in the non-cooperation and the Khilafat movements.

Although some Hindu leaders remained opposed to this, the noncooperation was successfully launched with the *hartal*.[253]

---

[251] Gandhi's non-cooperation was definitely viewed as the alternative. Shaukat Ali and other Khilafatist leaders urged Muslims to consider non-cooperation and to support it if they could not emigrate to Afghanistan. See *Hafeez Malik, Moslem Nationalism in India and Pakistan*, pp. 343ff.

[252] With the failure of the Hijrat movement to Afghanistan, Muslim leaders realised non-cooperation was the only way left for them. While Gandhi fully supported and was anxious to launch the non-cooperation movement with the scheduled *hartal* on 1st August, Pandit Malaviya attempted to pressure Gandhi to postpone his movement. Malaviya urged Hindus not to join the *hartal* on 1st August. Gandhi was under tremendous pressure from the Muslim leaders as well who threatened Muslim withdrawal from Gandhi's movement if Gandhi postponed the *hartal*.

[253] One thing that contributed to the success of the *hartal* was the death of Bal Gangadghar Tilak on the eve of the launching of non-cooperation. All over India a sense of urgency prevailed to join the *hartal* at least to honour the memory of Bal Gangadhar Tilak. See Minault, p. 108.

Maulana Abul Kalam Azad had been invited in February, 1920 to preside over the Bengal Provincial Khilafat session in Calcutta. Azad gave a very detailed exposition of the meaning of the Caliphate in Islam. It was an institution that would give the *da'wa* (invitation) to Islam—a chance to attain salvation. The purpose was to establish on the Earth a just society in which there was peace. It would be a time and place where Allah's Word would spread, and for that it was necessary for the Caliph to have temporal power. Azad said it made little sense that the British government allowed Muslims to pray but did not allow temporal power[254] to the Caliphate, which was a religious duty. Azad did not understand the attitude of the government which allowed them the pilgrimage but forced the Caliph to hand over the pilgrimage places to non-Muslims. He urged Muslim friendship with Hindus because they lived in peace with Muslims but not with the British government because they invaded Muslim lands and threatened the religion.[255] Also, Maulana Mahmud al-Hasan *(Shaykh al-Hind)*, ever since his return from internment in Malta, remained very active.[256] Upon his release, Muslims in Bombay pledged to him that they would work for freedom in India. They said it was obligatory upon them because the Europeans had adopted a policy of hostility towards the Caliphate [257] He died after being elected *Sadr al-Mudarris* (Chief Professor) at Deoband. Muslims in India wanted to elect him as the Imam or *Shaykh al-Islam* for the

---

[254] Abul Kalam Azad, *Masala-e-Khilafat wa Jazira-e-Arab*. It is important to note that in Azad's explanation, it was essential for the Caliph to have temporal power. They found a reason in the *Shari'a* to defend this institution of the Caliphate, threatened by the world events.

[255] Ibid.,

[256] Mahmud al-lasan was dying of cancer and had only five more months of his active life left. Mahmud al-Hasan utilised this fully, travelling extensively and talking vigorously about the Khilafat issue.

[257] See *Naqsh-i-Hlnd*, 2:235-236.

whole of India. When he died, he had already presided at the second annual session of *Jami`at al-Ulama*[258].

After *Shaykh al-Islam*'s death, among the candidates for the status of Imam was Maulana Abul Kalam Azad. He was not successful, since he did not have a broad enough base of support among Muslims. But Abul Kalam Azad had a clearly planned strategy if he were to be elected. He wanted to unite with Hindus and oust the British government from India.[259]

The most successful group among religious orders were the Sufis in Sind; they became a formidable force there. The Sufi leaders said that for Islam to flourish it must be independent and not be subjugated because it was important to wield political power for the defense of religion. This was an echo of Jamal al-Din al-Afghani's theory of *Dar al-Islam* we have already seen. His political awakening, which had dawned at the beginning of the century, evolved into a mass movement by 1921.

In a special session of the Indian National Congress was held in September 1920. In this session, Gandhi and other leaders, after arguments and disagreements, finally agreed to support Muslims fully in their Khilafat agitation. They also fully and officially adopted, again after much discussion, the policy of non-cooperation with the British government.

By 1921, the Khilafat agitation reached its height as the anti-British movement had gathered full momentum. They raised successful funds and secured new memberships. Muslims were particularly active in achieving mass mobilisation. Their most active members were the Ali brothers, Hakim Ajmal Khan, Dr. Mukhtar Ahmad *Ansari*, Maulana Abdul Bari and Maulana

---

[258] see *Tazkira*, pp. 283-286. Also see *Naqsh,* 2 : 235-236.
[259] See *Zikr,* p,. 24. See also Minault, p. 104. Mian, *Ulema-e-Haq,* 1:209-13.

Abul Kalam Azad. The steps they took to achieve this are worth reviewing.

First, they started enlisting student cooperation. The first institution to respond was Aligarh. The most important thing for teachers and students to do was to withdraw from government schools and colleges. The Ali brothers and Gandhi addressed students on October 12, 1920. Students took action at once, giving the school board an ultimatum of their boycott by October 29th, 1920. On the same day, Muhammad Ali announced the formation of a completely independent Muslim University, *Jami'a Millia Islamia.* This university was inaugurated in the Aligarh College Masjid. Shaykh al-Hind gave a *khutba*, in which he emphasised it was a religious duty not to cooperate with the British government because of its conduct towards the Caliph (and Islam in general). He advised them to follow their consciences, not their parents, when it came to support the obligatory Islamic cause. He also hoped the curriculum of the new University would be combined with the curriculum of Deoband and the English education of Aligarh.[260]

Muhammad Ali began teaching in the new university he opened. It became a training ground for political operations but also gave instruction on religious aspects of the Khilafat movement. Students discussed about Indian freedom and noncooperation with the British government. Students also propagated to other colleges in Lahore and other places. Calcutta Madrasa also joined in. Students in the new university had become an important part of the Khilafat agitation. Gandhi and Nehru tried the same tactics with the Hindu university and colleges, but they were not very successful.[261]

Second, from the group of these students, some were selected into the Khilafat and Volunteer corps. Their job was

---

[260] See Mahmud al-Hasan, *Khutba-i-Sadarat aur Fatwa-i-Tark-i-Mawalat.* See also Abdul Gaffar Madhauli, *Jamia ki Kahani.*

[261] See Minault, pp. 108ff.

to propagate the Khilafat agitation and to control the crowds. Volunteer groups had existed in India even before the Khilafat agitation. We have examples in Gokhal's Servants of Indian Society in 1905. Then we have the *Anjuman-e-Khuddam-e-Kaaba,* the organisation we saw in the previous chapter. What was new in the Khilafat movement was that it was organised this time not only for social for reasons but also for political and religious reasons. Also, because it was on a national scale, it grew rapidly and extensively. Its partisans helped patrol the city on the Caliphate Day. They organised processions and speeches and supervised the processions to prevent them from becoming unruly. By 1920, they had become openly political and had their own volunteers1 uniforms—complete with khaki outfit, Fez caps, and Arab-style robes.[262] These volunteers were moved by public enthusiasm and cheers and moral support they received. [263]

Third, the *'ulama* were mobilised. They used all their influence to reach *ijma'*(consensus among the *'ulama*) in order to issue a *fatwa* that favoured non-cooperation. They found more courage because the *Shaykh al-Hind* had returned from internment in Malta. The *'ulama* held the view that anyone cooperating with the British government was an infidel himself. Abdul Bari mentioned this in his various sermons. Their one-page *fatwa,*[264] signed and sealed by five-hundred *'ulama,* was proscribed. The *fatwa* carried five clauses:

(1)   It is forbidden in shari`a to be members of Government councils.

(2)   It is forbidden to plead cases in Government courts.

---

[262]   See Minault, p.116 ff. See the photograph in Minault, facing page 120.

[263]   See Jawaharlal Nehru, *Autobiography*, pp. 69, 77-78.

[264]   See *'Ulama-i Hind ka Muttafiq Fatwa,* Proscribed Material, Entries numbers 1495-1497. Also *Muttafiqa Fatwa-e-ulema-e-Hind* (Bombay: Central Khilafat Committe [I9201). App. 5.

(3) It is forbidden to receive education in Government Schools or Colleges aided by the Government.

(4) It is forbidden to hold honorary magistracy and other honorary ranks and titles given by the Government.

(5) All the Government services from which the Government receives help are forbidden. It is a serious sin to serve especially in the army and in the police, because they are duty bound to shoot their brothers, whereas Allah refuses to lift a weapon against a Muslim.

(1) Sarkar-i Hind ki Konsilon ki membri shar'an haram hai

(2) Hindustan ki sarkari adalaton me wikaalat karna haram hai

(3) Sarkar-i yaa na sarkar-i madrasaon me ta'alim hasil karna haram hai

(4) Anareri majistry, azasi uhde-u-khitabat-i atia gavament rakhna haram hai

(5) Sarkar ki jumla mulazamaton jin se oos ki madad hoti hai, khususan polis aur fauji mulazamaton qat'an haram hai.

Interestingly, the same was announced by the non-*'ulama* leaders including Gandhi.[265] Indeed, if this was taken far, it would have serious repercussions. The British government became very concerned and had no objection for the pro-government agents, the "Aman Sabha" and the "Liberal League" to publish a counter *fatwa* discouraging people to

---

[265] See Bamford, *Histories of the Non-Co-Operation and Khilafat Movements*, pp. 162-163.

abide by the *Muttafiq Fatwa* of the *'ulama*. In reply to this, the *Jamiat-al-'ulama-al-Hind* issued another *fatwa* which was also proscribed.[266]

The *'ulama* began a campaign for separate Shari'a courts. In addressing the *'ulama* the Shaykh al-Hind appealed for the defense of Islam at all costs. The rest of the *'ulama* agreed and signed another *fatwa* to fully support the Khilafat leaders' noncooperation programme. The *'ulama* had become more politically outspoken.

Fourth, the Indian National Congress and the Khilafat organisations expanded at the village level. Gandhi and the Ali brothers received full support wherever they went. The support did not come only from the common people. Lawyers, teachers and professionals also joined in the Khilafat agitation. The British government started arresting Muslim journalists on charges of inciting violence. The three journalists arrested were Zafar Ali Khan of *Zamindar*, Zafar Ali Mulk of *An Nazir* and Tajuddin, editor of *Taj*. Muslims were singled out as the agitators. Gandhi took this to be the British government tactic to upset the Hindus harmonious relations with Muslims and said

---

[266] This counter *fatwa* from the *Jamiat-al-' ulama-al-Hind* read in part These associations, the *'Aman Sabha* and the 'Liberal League' etc., are the names of associations created by the Government agents for the purpose to suppress the Noncooperation movement and to weaken the Indians' religious demands . . . It is for this reason that the *Jamiat-al-'ulama-al-Hind* have decreed and made it incumbent not only upon Muslims but upon all . . . to abide by the *fatwa*. (Yeh associanon 'L i b e r a l League 'aur 'Aman Sabha 'waghayra ke namon se sarkar-i afsaraan ke zer-Ihidayat is gharaz se qaim ki jaa rahi hai ke Tehrik-i Nancoopera tion ko dabaya jawe aur Hindus taneon ki mazhabi mu talaba t ko kamzor kiya jawe . . . is wajeh se Jamiat-al'ulama-al-Hind nah siraf Musalmanon ko bal ke am . . . par ye *fatwa* w a j i b qarar kiya hai). See Proscribed Material, Entry number 1491. See App. 6.

that the British government was inherently satanic".[267] In order to by-pass the government institutions, national schools, law enforcing bodies and even arbitration courts were set up.

Fifth, *Swadeshi* activity was promoted.

Sixth, in the agrarian disputes, the farmers were encouraged to form *Kisan* (farmers) groups to deal with agrarian disputes.

Seventh, Gandhi promoted weaving and hand spinning wheels to boycott foreign cloth. In this regard, full support came from the leadership of the Deoband *'ulama*, Sayyid Husayn Ahmad Madame[268] and also from Maulana Abul Kalam Azad. It was significant that both of these leading personalities actively supported the boycott of foreign merchandise. Later, Madame produced a forty-two page booklet in which he recounted the important role played by the *'ulama* of the *Jamiat-al-'ulama-al-Hind* in promoting the boycott of foreign merchandise and their support in the Khilafat movement. Both Madani's writings and Azad's were proscribed. Madani wrote:

When the white, allied governments of Europe decided to eliminate the Turkish government and to destroy the institution of the Islamic Caliphate, and also to occupy the holy land of Arabia, the leaders of the *Jamiat-al-'ulama-al-Hind* showed their foresight. They decided to use the age-old Islamic tactic of boycott of goods and asked for noncooperation. For the guidance of Muslims everywhere, they decreed a unanimous *fatwa* making non-cooperation binding. Armed with this, the Khilafat committees and the leaders and workers of the Congress were prepared to fight with the government of the day . . . For the sacrifices of the Muslims of India and proper

---

[267] See Mohandas K. Gandhi, "Swaraj in One Year" in *The Khilafat Question*, vol. 10, pp. 3-7. See also 18:38.

[268] Sayyid Husayn Ahmad Madani succeeded as a leader of the Deoband seminary at the death of Sayyid Mahmud al-Hasan.

use of arms by the Turks, Allah saved the Turks from total annihilation. For this, Turks thanked the Muslims of India.

Jab keh Europe ki firangi taqaton ne Turkey hukwnat ko khatam kar dene aur Khilafat-i Islamiya ko tabaah kar dene ka faislah ar l i y a aur Hijaz-i Muqaddas par gabza jamaane ka irada kiya, oos waqt Jamiat-al-'ulama-al-Hind ke rahnumaon ne apni basirat se Tark-i Mawalat aur 'adam-i ta'awun ke qadimi Islami harbe ko ista'maal karne ka faislah k i y a. Aur Musamanon ki rehnumaai ke liye 'adam-i ta 'awun ke program ke m u t a l l i q ek muttafiqa fatwa tayyar kiya, jis ko le kar Khilafat kommitiaan aur Kangress ke rehnuma aur kaarkun hukumat-i waqt ke muqable me s a f-i ara huwa . . . Hindustani Musalmanon ki sarfarushi aur Turkon ki talwaar ke sariye Allah Paak ne Turkon ki hukumat ko fana hone se bacha liya, aur is silsile me Turkon ne Musalmanaan-i Hind ka shukriya ada kiya.[269]

Abul Kalam Azad's article appeared in his *al-Hilal*. Published under the title *Baikat* (Boycott), this was the fourth re-print and considered seditious by the British government and proscribed. In the article, he reminds Muslims in the strongest European aggression. Azad, as always, likes to seek support in what he quotes from the Qur'anic verses that he thinks are appropriate to the point he is making.

Azad begins with the Qur'anic verses and gives them an Arabic title, "*Yaa layta Qawmi Ya'lamun*" (Oh I wish my community knew). Azad appeals to Muslims not to consider the western Europeans as friends and to boycott any trade relationship with them. This article is certainly illuminating in several aspects:

First, it underscores how defeated and helpless Muslims had begun to feel as a result of fifty years of the very harsh socioeconomic conditions Muslims were put in following the

---

[269] See Sayyid Husayn Ahmad Madani, Proscribed Material, Entry number 1514.

troubles of the 1857 uprisings and the support Muslims gave to this movement.

Second, it points out the new awakening and demonstration of enthusiasm and concern for the protection of Muslim holy places (Makkah, Madina, Najaf, and Karbala) through financial support.

Third, the warm reception of such writing, and its being proscribed by the British government when it was printed for the fourth time in 1922 shows the support of Muslims to the Khilafat movement. They had begun to appreciate the seriousness of their perilous situation. They were reacting forcefully to the incident of the Kanpur massacre. They were also producing poems comparing their situation with Karbala's `Ashura` tragedy and were coming into an open confrontation with the authorities at the peak moment of the Khilafat issue.

One can read, for example, the laments of Maulana Abul Kalam Azad.

From where can I get a lamenting sound that would reach the hearts and minds of four-hundred million (Muslims) waking them up from their oblivion? . . . (they are like those) travellers in a ship which is caught up in a heavy sea-storm and the end of their life is approaching fast, yet they are asleep in their oblivion; or (if they know they are sinking) they feel helpless and cry to themselves; or helplessly look at one another and their feet show no sign of any movement (as if they are paralysed with fear!). They demonstrate no courage and they lack any will to act (and save themselves) . . . (more) . . . In this regard, the first step they-Muslims) should take is to boycott, as far as possible, all merchandise that is being manufactured and has its origin in Europe . . . (more) . . . Today, all of the Christian world is accusing us (Muslims) of barbarism, blood-shed, murder and troublemaking. They are succeeding in this false propaganda against us . . . We always protected

Christian places of worship. We protected Churches more than we did our own Mosques, we even gave up lands reserved for building Mosques for the building of Churches. But today, our Mosques of Tripoli and Gallipoli are not safe from the boots of invading Christians. Half of the minaret of the Mosque of Gauhar Shah in the city of Mashhad has already been bombarded by the invading Christian army . . . (more) . . . Muslims must always remember that they are being downtrodden and made to feel worthless, and in spite of all the manipulations of the West, using their internal and external sources, to instill in Muslims' minds the feeling that they are ineffective and paralysed, Muslims should remember that their numbers (in India) are in excess of seventy million. This is the largest of any land that is populated by the followers of Islam . . . Muslims (must not forget) that they have lost their rule only recently. Therefore, in spite of their decline and feelings of total helplessness and despondency, they are not totally hopeless. They have money. They have education and with the rude new awakening (that the British and their allies are set out to destroy the Caliphate and wipe out Islam), they should know that while the Turks have the major responsibility to provide protection to the first Tenet of Islam (*Tawhid*, or Sovereignty of Allah as the only true Sovereign-King), Muslims in India are no less responsible to provide protection and defence to the holy places (Makkah, Madina, Najaf, Karbala, and Mashhad) so that the Islamic shari'a codes are not violated. In this regard, their responsibility exceeds to the Islamic lands because of their sheer numbers in India, largest of any other Islamic lands. . . . You may say that Muslims have already demonstrated in a very short time, their enthusiasm and their concern for the fate of the Ottoman empire by collecting millions of Rupees. What more could they possibly do? I will reply by saying that you still have a lot more to offer, provided you know, and are aware of all your capabilities when it comes to defend your own faith . . . Let the love of Allah and His *Rasul* (Messenger) take precedence over your personal self-interest. Certainly those who contributed money were motivated by their heart-felt concern for the cause and that is indeed valuable. Such concern only gives hope in the time of doom. The provision of financial assistance was the first and foremost form of *jihad* of which Muslims are aware. But my question is not: What has been done so far? I would like to ask: Have they done all they could possibly do? Financial assistance will certainly help purchase the essential supplies for the treatment of the injured Turks. But it will do nothing to change the power of that sword which keeps inflicting new wounds every day . . . (more) . . . The enthusiasm and concern are the foundation for action. But mere shedding tears (and feeling helpless) never led to any conquest. Believe me, all Christian Europe is now decided to destroy Islam, and our petitions and resolutions are of no avail to this world.

Main wo sur kahan se laun jiski aawaaz chaalis krore dilon ko khwaab-i ghaflat se bedar kar de? . . . Us kishti-e tufani ke maayus musafir jinki maut-o-hayat ke akhri lamhe jald jald guzar rahe hain, aur wo bekhabar hain, ya khamosh rota hain ya mayusi se chap-o rast nigran. magar na inke hathon me i z t a r a b hai aur na paw me harkat, na himmaton me iqdam hai aur na aradon me amal ka walwalwala . . . is silsile men pehla kam ye hai ke hatt-al-inkam tama European mal-i tajarat aur mas nuat ko bikat kar den . . . laikin aaj tamam masihi dunya hum per wahsha t— Okhun-rezi aur qatl-o fasad ka buhtan lagane me kamyab ho rahi hai. Ham ne Roz-i-Awwal se unki ma'bodon aur girjon ko apni masaajidon ki hifaazat se kam nahin samjha. Aur ek martaba damashq ki Masjid ki tamir shuda zmin dedi taa-ke is par Girja ban jaye, Laikin aaj Taraplas aur Galipoli ki MasjidonMasjidon-ki Mihrab aur Mimbar bhi saleeb paraston ke hamlawar booton se mehfuz nahin hai, aur Mashhad ki Masjid-i Gohar Shah ka nisf Gumbad topon ki golabari se gira diya gaya hai . . . Hindustan ke Muslamanon ne khwah ki tna hi apne t a i n zalil aur be-haqiqat samajh l i y a ho, aur khwah dakhl aur kharji Shayatin-ki waswasa-andazion ne ki tna hi inko muattal aur majboor hone ka t a q l i n d i l a diya ho, l a i k i n inko yad rakhna chahie, keh inki taadad saat crore se muj-jawaz h a i, aur woh

aaj aprawan-i Islam ki sab se bari taadad hai. Jo zamin ke
kisi aur turre men abad hai, inko awan-i Hukumat se nikle
huwe abhi ziada zamana nahin guzra h a i, aur bewajud har tareh
ke tanazzal ke ab bhi dolat aur talim aur a l a l khalus ne
bedari aur apne masaib ke mahsoos kame men un mawamat ke
musalmanon se be-nisbatan behtar halat rakhte hain, jahan ab
tak Islami hukumat baqi h a i, is liye agar aaj H i f z Kalema-
Tawhid-o-Baqa, Balad-Muqaddassa Qiyam-o Shumaar-o naamus
s h a r i a t-i Islamia ki sab se zyada zimmedari Turkon ke zim-me
hai. Kyun ke inke hathon me Talwar hai. To yaqin ki jiye, keh
Muslamanan-i Hind ke zim me bhi i n s e kam nahin hai. Kyun ke
Inki tadaad tamam dunya ki Islami abadiyun me sab se zyada
hai. Aap kahenge keh Musalmanon ne chand mahinon ke andar kis
qadar josh-o-iqtarab ka i z h a r kiya aur kis mustaadi se lakhon
rupiya Turkie ki aanat mein faraham dar liya. Is se ziyada aur
in ke bas me kiya hai? Laikin mai kahunga keh bas me to sab
kutch hai, bashate ke woh apni quwwat ka andaaza karen.
Kalima-i Tawhid ki h i f a z a t keh liye 00th khare hon aur apne
nafs keh muqable me Allah aur uske Rasul ki muhabbat ko t a r j i h
de. Yaqinan woh tes jo dard-i Islami k i inhone apne d i l me
paida ki, nihayat qimti hai. Woh iqtarab aur hajan jo inhone
is waqt zahir k i y a, is alam-yaas me bhi unmrid ka payam hai aur
rupiya ki farahami bhi ek awwalin jihad-mali tha, j i s se woh
ghafaf na rahai, laikin mera sawal ye nahin hai keh inhone kya
kutch kiya? balke main puchna chahta hun ke jo kar sakte the
woh kiya ke nahin? Rupiya bhej kar aap zakhmi Turkon ki
marham patti ka zuroor samaan kar sate hain laikin oos talwar
ke hamle ki quwwat par t u kutch asar nahin dal sakte, jo nai
nai zakham paida kar rahi hai. Josh-o iztarab bunyad kar hai,
l a i k i n siraf aansu baha kar tun kisi fauj ne mulk fteh nahin
kiya. Yaqin ki jiye, keh taman masihi yurup ab Islam ke fana
kar dene ke liye aakhri i t t i f a q kar chuka hai aur arazdashton
aur rezolushanon se dunya me kabhi kam nahin n i k l a haie[270]

---

[270] See Abul Kalam Azad, Baikat, Proscribed Material, Entry number
1411. See Appendix 7.

Once all these steps were taken, then the next stage would be civil disobedience, boycott of the army, and boycott of police and taxes. Gandhi hoped that the British government machinery would falter and *swaraj* would be achieved within a year. At the same time, Gandhi wanted all these steps to be followed without any violence whatsoever. Gandhi had become nervous, however, because he thought not all Muslims would fully cooperate with his totally non-violent methods. This was so because Muslim emotions were running very high, especially at the humiliating Peace terms.

During the summer of 1921, disagreement over the issue of non-violence developed between Gandhi and Abdul Bari and the Ali brothers. Also, rumours about a Muslim invasion from Afghanistan, to oust the British government from India and help Muslims, triggered old fears in the minds of Hindus. This led to some inter-communal riots in Malabar.

CHAPTER FOUR:

INDIAN MUSLIM THEORISTS OF THE KHILAFAT

When the Grand National Assembly in Turkey abolished the Caliphate in 1924, the Khilafat movement in India was threatened with collapse. This was the demise of an institution that had its roots in the deeply held Sunni Islamic theology. [271]Muslims in India, as seen from the Proscribed Material, a deep feeling of despondency had set in. The Khilafat movement, launched in 1919, had a clearly defined purpose. Its leader, Maulana Muhammad 'Ali, stated that it was launched not for aggression or even for the defence of Turkey, but just for the defence of our faith.[272] It was to guarantee continuance of its mandate over the Jazirat al-'Arab, and as well for it to remain, as always, the guardian of holy places.[273] It was launched, as we have already seen in earlier chapters, partly in response to the pan-Islamic ideas of Jamal al-Din al-Afghani. A new dimension from al-Afghani's ideas, *Dar al-Islam* versus *Dar al-Harb*, had been added to the Khilafat movement when it became apparent that the British government would not deliver on the promise given Muslims during the war. The edict issued by Abdul Bari and supported by prominent 'ulama from the Khilafatist leaders declared India *Dar al-Harb*, and the

---

[271] Of the two branches in Islam, the Sunnis believe in the concept of the Caliphate. The Shi`as believe in the concept of the Imamate.

[272] Afzal Iqbal, *Select Writings and Speeches of Maulana Mohamed A l i*, Vol. If, pp. 6-7.

[273] Indian Muslims had always demanded mandates not only over Mecca, Madina and Jerusalem but also over the Shi'a holy places in Karbala, Najaf and Mashhad.

obligatory hijra to *Dar al-Islam* had also failed.[274] While the Khilafat Movement united Hindus and Muslims temporarily, this unity suffered a severe setback with the Moplah rebellion[275] in 1921 and then the Chauri Chaura incident. The Moplah Rebellion was in Malabar. Moplas, a community of Muslims of mixed Arab and Indian descent, fell upon Hindus. The Chauri Chaura[276] incident was the fire-bombing of a police station in Uttar Pradesh killing 21 officers. These events resulted in Gandhi's calling off his noncooperation movement. Gandhi thus withdrew his support for Muslims in their Khilafat movement.

The abolition of the Caliphate and the incidents mentioned in the above paragraph meant more communal riots, which continued in India unabated. [277]Worse still, Hindus organised the Shuddhi (purification)[278] and Sangathan (ethnic struggle)[279]

---

[274] See Sikandar Hayat, *Aspects of Pakistan Movement*, p. 11 ff. See also Wahid-u-Zaman, *Towards Pakistan*, p.28. See also T. Morrison, in Sir John Cumming, ed., *Political India* 1832-1932, p. 97.

[275] The Moplah Rebellion was a communal explosion in Malabar. The communal violence that ensued was fierce, and martial law had to be imposed as the army was called in to restore order. See K. K. Aziz, *The Making of Pakistan: A Study in Nationalism*, p. 37.

[276] 1n February 1922, Gandhi s "National Volunteers" were responsible for the killing of twenty-one police officers working in their police station in Chauri Chaura when a petrol bomb was thrown in. The fire soon engulfed the station. See Edward Thompson and G.T. Garratt, *Rise and Fulfilment of British Rule in India*, p. 618.

[277] See Sharif al Mujahid, Communal Riots, "in A History of Freedom Movement", Vol. IV, part 11, pp. 42-89.

[278] Movements designed to reclaim Muslims back to Hinduism since Hindus believed Muslims in India were all Hindus before they got converted to Islam.

[279] While it is true that the shuddhi and sangathan movements disturbed Muslims in India, Swami Shraddhananda, a driving force in the pan-lindu shuddhi and sangathan movements, explained in the special meeting of the Congress held in Delhi in September 1923 that the responsibility of some of the communal violence

movements, in which Muslims would be forced to reject Islam and accept Hinduism. Muslims took these two movements[280] to intend the complete annihilation of Muslims in India. Riots increased, and there was hardly a day that passed in which there was no communal violence reported from somewhere in India.

But the abolition of the Caliphate also meant that "Sunni political thought reached a turning point . . . and was the apogee of a long period of intellectual ferment among Muslims which had started at the end of the eighteenth century.[281] It precipitated vigorous debates between traditionalists and modernists. Some synthesis might have resulted from all this, but as Hamid Enayat tells us, polemics to the advantage of traditionalists pushed the Muslim mind in the direction of an alternative to the Caliphate . . . the call for the Islamic state.[282] If the Muslim mind (i.e., Muslim intellectual and political leaders) was envisioning a supra-national Muslim state, in which Muslims were distinctly superior with the Caliph enjoying total temporal authority, then a perception like this had become outdated. That is because the pan-Islamic ideas of al-Afghani and Abduh had become outdated by the time the Caliphate was abolished. It seemed impossible to have a State in which a Muslim Caliph enjoyed complete temporal authority. The new challenge Muslims were facing, as it appears, was how to deal with the concept of a modern westernised state which was based on the will of the people. Defeated Turkey, holding within itself the seat of the Caliph, responsible for the defence of faith and welfare of Muslims all over the world, could never provide

---

should not be attributed to the shuddhi and sangathan movements alone. Muslim Maulvis had their share in creating troubles at some places. See J.T.F. Jordens, *Swami Shtadhananda*, pp. 138-151.

[280] It is to be noted that these movements were not widespread throughout India. Sangathan remained mainly around the Punjab area.

[281] see Hamid Enayat, *Modern Islamic Political Thought*, p. 52.

[282] Ibid., p. 52.

government to all the Muslim nations of the world. There was a dilemma in the constitution accepted by the Turkish National Assembly in January 1921 declaring sovereignty belonging unconditionally to the people of Turkey. This was based on the principle that people would control their own destiny, in person and in fact.[283]

The most significant argument, for the purpose of this thesis, is in a document that the Grand National Assembly published. It states why it was correct, even from the point of view of Islamic Shari'a, to do away with the institution of the Caliphate and replace it with the State. The Assembly clearly did not consider the Abbasid caliphate to be totally legitimate and even if the pro-Caliphate opinions of the classical theorists were considered to be applicable, they would only apply to people of their time. However, the Islamic Shari'a had clearly provided a provision-in fact an Islamic principle-of a *shura* (consultative committee), which would be totally authorised to make decisions for the proper conduct of the nation's affairs. Withdrawing the political functions of the Caliph was one such decision taken up by the assembly. In this they relied and quoted persistently on the resources of Shari'a . . . and canonical maxims prescribing justice, expediency, common sense and the simplicity of good religion.[284]

This was not the first time in Islamic history that Muslims had faced the dilemma of the collapse of the Caliphate. We have already seen in Chapter One that with the Mongol invasion in 1258, the Abbasid caliphate collapsed and the Muslim world went without a Caliph for three-and-a-half years until the Mamluk dynasty in Cairo reinstated the cousin of the last Abbasid caliph, because they wanted to achieve legitimacy in their rule over their domains.[285]

---

[283] See Arnold, p. 209.

[284] See Enayat, p. 56. quoted from "Califat et souverainte nationale" in *Revue du Monde Musulman*, 59 (1925).

[285] A. Suyuti, *History of Caliphs,* tr. H. S. Jarel, pp. 500-501.

It is interesting, though very ironic, that Indian Muslims, who were so vocal in their appeals to their colonial masters to preserve and honor the Ottoman Caliph, were also, at least indirectly, the cause of its abolition. In a special appeal the two distinguished Muslim leaders-the Shi'a Amir Ali and the Isma'ili leader, the Agha Khan-made was a text they published in Istanbul in November 1923. The text pointed out the significance of the institution of the Caliphate because of the confidence and esteem it commanded upon the Muslim nations and therefore the strength and dignity it imparted to the Turkish state. It was precisely such protests that tightened Mustapha Kemal's resolve to remove the Caliphate.[286] It may also be, as W.C. Smith points out, that the Turks felt angry that the protest against their action was made by such non-Sunni personalities because Amir Ali was a Shi'a and the Aga Khan a Khoja.[287]

Muslims in India must have been stunned at the decision taken by Turkey's National Assembly. They did not, however, turn away from the concept of the Caliphate in which they so strongly believed. What was needed was re-modeling their thought process so that the concept could fit in with the new situations of the twentieth century. They needed to search for a proper Islamic solution vis-a-vis the modern age. We shall see how this thought process was changed in India as Indian Muslims re-aligned their thoughts to fit the newly emerged concept of "nationalism" the early twentieth-century India.

Among the Khilafatist leaders, Abul Kalam Azad was fully conversant with Islamic theology. Azad did not find it difficult to agree with the argument put forward by Mustapha Kemal that the Caliph cannot be compared with the Pope. The concept of the Papacy in Christianity differed from the concept of the Caliphate because, as Mustapha Kemal put it:

---

[286] See Bernard Lewis, *The Emergence of Modern Turkey,* pp. 259-260.

[287] W.C. Smith, *Modern Islam in India,* (London, 1946), p. 206.

"The notion of a single Caliph, exercising supreme religious authority over all Muslim people, is one which has come out of books, not reality. The Caliph has never exercised over the Muslims a power similar to that held by the Pope over the Catholics. Our religion has neither the same requirements, nor the same discipline as Christianity"[288].

While Azad agreed with most of what Mustapha Kemal was saying, he disagreed with the point that the Caliph did not have the authority to demand obedience from all Muslims. Azad believed that obedience to the Caliph was binding on all Muslims because "spiritual leadership (in Islam) was the due of Allah and His Prophet alone."[289]

But not all Muslims agreed that the Ottoman emperor was the rightful Caliph for Muslims in India. We have already seen in earlier chapters that from among the moderate 'ulama, at least Sir Sayyid, did not agree that the Ottoman emperor's Caliphate extended to include allegiance from Indian Muslims. It seems to me that Sir Sayyid was already exerting himself in *ijtihad* and had concluded in his own words: "The times are constantly changing, and the method suited to the past is no longer suited to the present . . ."[290]

Like Iqbal, who was to follow him a generation afterwards, Sir Sayyid believed that Islam was never stagnant. It was compatible with all progress that science and reason were making. Sir Sayyid advised Muslims to examine critically and rationally issues of social ethics facing them every day so as

---

[288] Enayat, pp. 53-54. See also http://www.scribd.com/doc/80754308/ The-Caliphate-Question-The-British-Government-and-Islamic-Governance.

[289] See A shfaque Husain, *The Quintessence of Islam*, p. 16.

[290] See Hayat, "Syed Ahmed Khan and the Foundation of Muslim Separatist Political Movement in India" in Pakistan Journal of Social Sciences, 8: 1-2 (Jan-Jul-Dec 1982), p. 38.

to conform with the true religion of Islam.[291] That Sir Sayyid was exerting himself in *ijtihad* is clearly seen when he criticized contemporary Muslims who were still clinging to those social values in Islam that were old and needed to be looked at afresh in the light of modem progress. He said that the old method was like a broom of which the string that binds the twigs is broken and therefore the twigs have fallen apart "and cannot be reunited unless a fresh cord is provided.[292]

In all this, Sir Sayyid insisted Islam had compatibility with modern thinking. In other words, the rational thinking he was demanding from Muslims would not be at the expense of Islam. Rather, it would make Muslims appreciate Islam even more. Should Muslims forget Islam because of higher education, then he would have no relationship with them because the only thing "that binds you and me and the rest of the Muslim community is that of God and His Prophet . . . '[293]

---

[291] See Aziz Ahmed, *Islamic Modernism*, p. 32. See also Ishtiaq Husain Qureshi, *The Muslim Cornunity of the Indo-Pakistan Sub-Continent (610-1947)*, p. 266.

[292] It must have been also by way of *ijtihad* that Sir Sayyid advised Muslims to remain loyal to the British rule and not to oppose it. This he concluded from the rules of jihad. He said that Jihad became incumbent upon Muslims only when Muslims were denied peace and were denied practising their faith. Since there was no fear of persecution under the British rule it was incumbent upon Muslims to be loyal to the British. Another ijtihad of Sir Sayyid is seen in the field of education. He insisted on Westernised education but warned in the same breath never to ignore their traditional curricula. Education was necessary for Muslims, he believed, because only then would they be able to know what their rights were and only then would they feel confident enough to demand them. See Syed Ahmed, The Present State of Indian Politics: Speeches and Letters, p. 77.

[293] See Hayat, p. 37.

It appears that Sir Sayyid was preparing Muslims for the demand for a separate state that they would have to make of the British government at some future date. His preparation for this was through reform, exerting ijtihad. These reforms included first, to bridge the gap between Muslims and the British authority in the difficult situation Muslims found themselves in after the 1857 uprising. Second, he explained to Muslims that it was in keeping with Islamic tradition to be loyal to the British government. Third, he insisted on awareness in Muslim minds and this he firmly believed would be achievable only through education. For Muslims to have their own institution of learning, he even established a college in Aligarh. Fourth, he never accepted that Muslims could co-exist with a Hindu majority. As a matter of fact, he promoted in Indian Muslims a feeling that they were a distinct community. In one of his public meetings, he even declared that when Muslims came together in any congregation, the feeling of one nation for Islam takes birth in our hearts . . . an involuntary emotion . . . to the thought

"our nation! our nation! . . . This is not merely my assertion; I trust that all here will acknowledge this truth. If you will reflect the principles of our religion, you will see the reason why our Prophet ordered all the dwellers in neighbourhoods to meet five times a day for prayers in the mosque, and why the whole town had to meet together on Fridays in the city mosque, and in Bid all the people had to assemble. The reason was that the effect of gathering should influence us all, and create a national feeling among those present, and show them the glory of nation.[294]

It is clear that he was telling Muslims that the "nationalist" basis of their well-being was Islam. Indeed, he also demanded their first loyalty to Islam because Islam alone bestowed upon them membership in the Muslim nation.[295] He was instilling

---

[294] See Ahmed, *The Present State of Indian Politics,* p. 94.
[295] Hayat, pp. 38-39.

in the Muslim mind that Muslims are a nation of their own. Anyone who joins the fold of Islam becomes part of that nation. Progress is achievable but not at the expense of Islam. It is only if progress is achieved by adhering to Islam that it would mean the true fostering of Islam and its national wellbeing.

A nation cannot constitute a nation in real sense unless all individuals joining the fold of Islam, together constitute a nation for Muslims.[296]

Some scholars have presented Sir Sayyid as a "separatist" only because he was disappointed with Hindus who were seeking to do away with the Urdu language only to replace it with Hindi.[297]

Also, some scholars have felt that Sir Sayyid developed "separatist" ideas because of the demands Hindus were making in the Congress simply because they were in the majority.[298]

The evidence that I have presented here shows otherwise. Sikandar Hayat presents him as a "Muslim separatist" who was presenting Muslims as a separate political group in Indian politics and was laying the foundation of a "Muslim separatist"

---

[296] G. Allana ed., *Pakistan Movement : Historic documents*, p. 1. See also "Pakistan Movement based on Islamic ideology", Business Recorder, http://www.brecorder.com/supplements/88/1166817/.

[297] It should be noted that although Hindi and Urdu are close in vocabulary and structure of their grammar, they are not in script. Muslims have felt Urdu and Farsi to be languages that were the accomplishments of the Islamic civilisation in India. While Farsi originated elsewhere it was used as an official language of the Mughal courts, Urdu was the language spoken most widely throughout India. Muslims in India always remained very sensitive in preserving their linguistic heritage.

[298] See Suchin Sen, *The Birth of Pakistan*, p. 42. See also S.K.Bhatnagar, *History of the M.A.O. College*, pp. 21-25.

political movement in India.[299] It is true from the evidence presented that Sir Sayyid was a "Muslim separatist" but the political movement in India, the foundation of which he was laying would never be of a secular character. Rather, he can be viewed as a Muslim reformer with a vision that would inspire Khilafatists and later members of the All India Muslim League that it was possible through exertion in *ijtihad* to align Muslims with modernity. Once this was achieved, Muslims would be in a position to use modern terminology and demand a nation. Whether by that he meant a "separate nation" in future or just a feeling of togetherness in which Islam was freely and fully practiced is open to question. He said once, "Remember, you have to live and die by Islam and it is in keeping up Islam that a nation is a nation."[300]

He was therefore laying a foundation on which (in less than generation after his death in 1898) Khilafatist leaders like Maulana Muhammad Ali, Maulana Shaukat Ali, Chaudhry Rahmat Ali, and its tacit supporters like Muhammad Iqbal and Muhammad Ali Jinnah would build the edifice of Muslim nationalism "and transform the separatist movement into a separate sovereign state of Pakistan.[301]

The most interesting reaction came from Muhammad Iqbal. Before we turn to his reaction, it is important to mention that although Iqbal did not take any significant active role in the Khilafat Movement, he fully supported the movement. It seems the only reason why Iqbal did not take any significantly active role was that he did not agree with the methodology adopted by the Khilafatist leaders.[302]

---

[299] See Hayat, p. 34.

[300] Allana, p. 1.

[301] Hayat, p. 34.

[302] Iqbal was appointed or elected a member of the Punjab Khilafat Committee but soon resigned because he did not approve of the methods adopted by the Khilafatist leaders. As a matter of fact, he considered it even dangerous for Muslims. In a letter he wrote to

Like Maulana Abul Kalam Azad, Iqbal had no difficulty agreeing with Turkey's National Assembly on the abolition of the Caliphate. Iqbal also agreed with the address Mustapha Kemal gave on the reasons why Turkey was taking this action. What is most interesting is that Iqbal analyzed the theological and philosophical aspects of Islam dealing with the position of the Caliphate in Islam and arrived at a very extra-ordinary conclusion: Iqbal believed that as a cultural movement, Islam always adopted a dynamic view and rejected the old, static view of the universe. He expounded this thesis by saying that external principles must never be understood to exclude possibilities of change. This was a divine gift and from the greatest signs of God. This movement of change in Islam is *ijtihad*. It means to "exert" and those who exert in *ijtihad* are shown the path to follow.[303] Thus, when a Companion of the Holy Prophet, Ma'ad, was appointed ruler from Yemen, in a dialogue that took place between him and the Prophet reportedly asked him how he would decide matters that would come up before him. When Ma'ad replied he would judge according to the Qur'an and the precedents set up by the Prophet, the Prophet asked him, "But if precedents fail?" To this question Ma'ad replied, "In that case, I will exert my own judgment." *Ijtihad*, therefore, is a necessary requirement. It has three degrees, complete authority, relative authority and special authority. This can be explained as follows:

M.N. Khan on 11 February 1920 he gave his reasons for resigning from the Khilafatist movement: "The way this (Khilafa) Committee was started, and the object some of its members had in view, the existence of this committee was in my opinion dangerous for the Muslims. See *Makatib i-Iqbal*, p. 27. See also S.A. Vahid, *Studies in Iqbal*, p. 268.

[303] Iqbal quoted this from the Qur'an: "Those who struggle (exert themselves in search of the Truth) for Us, We shall certainly show them Our paths (to follow). Verily Allah is with those who do good." Ch. 29:69.

(1) Complete authority is authority in legislation, which is confined only to the founders of Schools

(2) Relative authority is authority which is limited only to a particular school and the

(3) Special authority is authority relating to law applicable to a particular school left undetermined by its founders. Iqbal said that he would concern only with complete authority (number 1 above) and was astonished that although the process of *Ijtihad* existed as admissible by Sunni Islam,[304] in practice it has always been denied. This is in spite of the fact that its groundwork has been provided by the Qur'an, which provides a dynamic outlook on life. Iqbal blamed this attitude on the Mu`tazilites [305]the Sufi movement.

---

[304] The Shi'a school already has ijtihad in place. The Ayatullahs are really called the mujtahidin, those who continuously exert themselves to arrive at proper conclusion of issues presented to them. There is a proper doctrine in place regarding the *usul al-fiqh* (principles of jurisprudence) which an Ayatullah has to use to arrive at a conclusion of the problem he may be working on.

[305] Iqbal cited the *mihna* movement (inquisition) that took place in time of the 'Abbasid Caliph al-Mansur over the question of the eternity of the Qur'an. The Mu'tazilites denied it because they thought it was only another form of Christian belief of eternity of this world. Conservatives, on the other hand, thought that the Mu'tazilite movement could become a force of disintegration and danger to the stability of Islam as a social polity. They decided against any form of rationalism. The binding force was the Shari'a, and they made this as rigorous as possible. Iqbal believed Sufism came under influence of a non-Islamic character, purely on the speculative side. On its religious side it quibbled against the early 'ulema. Their emphasis on zahir and batin aspects created only indifference to all that applied to appearance, far from' reality. Therefore, their vision was blinded to Islam as a social polity. They decided against any form of rationalism.

Muslim states were left to these intellectuals mediocrities, whereas the masses of Islam blindly followed the schools. The destruction of Baghdad in the middle of the thirteenth century was a very severe blow. The 'ulama got busy in maintaining social order and organisation. It was a mistake, because, as Iqbal puts it, "in an over organised society the individual is altogether crushed out of existence.[306] Iqbal felt elated that Turkey, in deciding to abolish the institution of the Caliphate, was only reinforcing *ijtihad* and in fact broadening it with modem philosophical ideas. Like the Turks, he said, Indian Muslims will one day, have to re-evaluate their intellectual inheritance.

Iqbal rejected the ideas of the National Party in Turkey because their supreme interest was the state and not religion. As a structure of a religio-political system it is possible that Islam may permit t h i s but not the idea that the state is dominant and in fact rules the whole system embodied in Islam. This must not be allowed to be so because in Islam the spiritual and temporal are not distinct domains. In any case, any act, even if secular, is determined by the attitude of the mind of the one who acts. An act becomes temporal only if it is done "on a spirit if detachment from the infinite complexity of life behind it; it is spiritual if it is inspired by that complexity". [307]It was an ancient mistake arising out of bifurcating the unity of man into two separate realities when they have, in fact, a point of contact although in essence they are opposed to each

---

[306] Nevertheless, it produced thinkers like ibn Taymiyya, who was similar to thinkers like Muhammad ibn Tumart amidst the decay of Spain. Ibn Taymiyyavs movement, though inwardly conservative, at least had a spirit of freedom manifested in it. it vigorously rejected the finality of schools and insisted on private judgment and in matters of law falling back on the Sunna of the Prophet. See Allama Muhammad Iqbal, *The Reconstruction of Religious Thought in Islam,* 2nd ed. pp. 116-153.

[307] Iqbal, pp. 153-54.

other. In truth, matter is spirit in space-and-time reference. Therefore, as some Indian philosophers explain that the unity that we call "man" is body when we look at it as acting in regard to the external world;[308] it is mind or soul when we look at it as acting. Similarly, the essence of *Tawhid* as a working idea is in reality equality, solidarity and freedom. The Islamic state should therefore be an exertion in *ijtihad* to change these ideals into space-time forces. In that sense, Iqbal believed the rule of Islam can be called a theocracy,

"not in the sense that it is headed by [a Caliph calling himself] representative of God on earth who can always screen his despotic will behind his supposed infallibility. The critics of Islam have lost sight of this important consideration".[309]

Iqbal agreed with the Grand Vizier of Turkey, Said Halim Pasha, who insisted that Islam is always a harmony of idealism and positivism and therefore cannot have a fatherland just as there can never be English mathematics, German astronomy or French chemistry, so there cannot be Turkish, Arabian,

---

[308] See for example," Indian philosophy : 19th-and 20th-century philosophy in India and Pakistan" in http://www.britannica.com/ EBchecked/topic/285905/Indian-philosophy/12370

[309] Iqbal explained that Turkish nationalists could not understand that Islam was from the very beginning dealing with a society, having received from the Qur'an simple legal principles which, like the Twelve Tables of the Romans, carried great potentialities of expansion and development by interpretation. It could therefore never separate the Church from the State. Christianity was founded from the beginning as a monastic order in a profane world. It did not concern itself with politics or the civil unit. When the Romans accepted Christianity, the State and Church confronted each other "as distinct powers with interminable boundary disputes between them." See Iqbal, p. 155. See also "The Principle of Movement in the Structure of Islam", in http://www.witness-pioneer.net/ vil/Books/MI_RRTI/chapter_06.htm

Persian or Indian Islam. Modern ideas of national egoism were therefore only another form of barbarism. Iqbal said that the Vizier Pasha was concerned that these moral and social ideals of Islam had become de-Islamised to some extent either through local cultures or through pre-Islamic superstitions. Because of this, the ideals had become more in nationalistic terms rather than simply Islamic. It was like "the pure brow of tauhid has received more or less an impress of heathenism and the universal and impersonal character of the ethical ideals of Islam has been lost through a process of localization".[310]

We see from the above, therefore, that although Iqbal agreed with the abolition of the Caliphate, he agreed only if it was to be replaced by an Islamic polity through the process of *ijtihad*.

This is important, as we shall see him voicing this idea in the famous speech he was to give in Allahabad in 1930—then to the Indian Muslims asking them to demand a state of their own. Obviously, Iqbal wanted a state created through *ijtihad* that would replace the Caliph and be represented instead by an elected assembly. It appears to me that Iqbal, in considering the abolition of the Caliphate in Turkey, was already formulating ideas in his mind about the future in India, although it is not possible to say whether he had any idea at this point what form it could or should take. He believed, it appears, that through *ijtihad* the 'ulama in India might arrive at a solution different from Turkey's because the conditions and problems of Muslims in India were different. In any case, Iqbal wanted to stir the 'ulama into thinking because the new situation for Muslims in India (the collapse of the cc to the Hindus in the Congress. Among the important ones who defected (some sooner than others) to Jinnah's camp were:

---

[310] Ibid., p. 156.

(a) ASHRAF ALI THANAWI

A contemporary of Madani, Ashraf Ali Thanawi, unlike Madani, did not involve himself in politics. He believed that the 'ulama's role was not to be involved in politics because their role was in the field of education. He championed division of responsibilities and believed that civilisation demanded everybody play their own role in life because if everybody was doing the same work it would be very baffling.[311] He nevertheless raised serious objections to Madani's siding with the Congress. [312] He regarded Hindus as enemies worse than the British and said that *tark-i mawalat* should be with Hindus as well as the British because both were the infidels.[313]

After the Congress rule of the Provinces, Thanawi said that in his opinion it was fatal to side with the Congress. He said that it would be tantamount to religious suicide if Muslims remained joined with the Congress.[314] To Jinnah s great delight, he asked Muslims to disregard the Congress and join the League. His reasons were obvious: if Muslims joined the League be possible to defeat the Congress and it would be possible to bring about the reformation in the party. It does not appear that Thanawi was really convinced that Jinnah and his ilk could create an Islamic state that would perform the function of a Caliph. Thanawi considered the leaguers to be the *fasiq'o fujjar.*[315] (rebels of the Sharia). He believed, however, that even

---

[311] See Ashraf 'Ali Thanawi, *Al-afazat al Yawmiyah* 3: 210 ff.

[312] Madani, his alliance with the Hindus was necessary within Islam because to him Hindus were the neighbours of Muslims, and therefore had rights over Muslims even though they were non believers. See Malik, p. 2l9f

[313] See *al-afazt al-Yawmiyah,* 5: 242 ff.

[314] See M. Shafi, *Afadat-i Ashrafiyyah dar Masail-i Siyasiyah* (Deoband, Dar al-Isha'at, 1945), pp. 65 ff.

[315] Thanawi sent three separate delegations to Jinnah to ask him to change the image of the Leaguers so that there should be in the League visible manifestations of Islam. Jinnah was asked to show

though the Leaguers were "sinners" because of his belief that they were *fasiq'o fujjar* (rebels of the Shari'a), he believed that it was possible to convert them back to Islamic ways. If an Islamic state were to be created it would be required in Islam that only the ways of Allah should reign supreme in that state.[316]

Jinnah understood the concern of the 'ulama and knew that their support was absolutely vital if he was to be successful in attaining a Muslim state.[317] Jinnah also knew that there were 'ulama ready to dissent from supporting Madani and his call for mawalat with Hindus. Jinnah, therefore, appointed a league worker, Raghib Ahsan, to persuade the 'ulama in Calcutta to form an organisation of 'ulama that would champion the cause of the League among the Indian Muslim masses. This worked wonderfully well as the dissenting 'ulama joined themselves to form in 1937 a group they called *Jam'iyat-i 'Ulama-i-Islam*. Later in 1945, the nephew of Ashraf Ali Thanawi, Zafar Ahmad Thanawi, established it in Calcutta. Ashraf Ali Thanawi himself died in 1943.

(b) SHABBIR AHMAD USMANI

During the Khilafat days Shabbir Ahmad Usmani was one of the most outspoken members of the Khilafat movement. Like other Khilafatists, Usmani, too, worked zealously for the Congress. In those days Gandhi's Non-cooperation movement had joined with the Khilafat movement. Usmani had championed *tark i mawalat* with the British on behalf of

---

publicly that he and the leaguers were practicing Muslims. See, for example, Ashraf Ali Thanawi, *Khatab ba Muslim Lig* (Saharanpur: Majlis Da'awat al Haq, 1938), pp 2 f f.

[316] See *Taimir-i Pakistan aur 'ulama-i Rabbani*, p. 64.

[317] The trouble was that the Jam'iyat were propagating widely that the League did not have the support of the 'ulama. This was of great concern to Jinnah because the support from 'ulema had to be earned at any cost.

the *Jam`iat-al-'ulama-al-Hind.* [318]He converted to become pro-League for the same reasons that Ashraf Ali Thanawi converted, that is, he perceived that the Congress was insensitive to Muslims' demands. He believed that for Muslims to support the non-believers the Muslims should be in a dominant position. If asked why he then supported Hindus during the Khilafat days, he would reply by saying that the Khilafat was a Muslim cause. He was therefore strictly supporting the Muslim cause. If Hindus had joined this cause it was because they were promoting their cause by joining the Khilafat Movement.

In his arguments for joining the pro-league *'ulama*, it is very clear that he thought along the lines of Pakistan as an Islamic state that would function as the Caliph.[319] Usmani repeated frequently his notion that the government in Pakistan would be based on the Qur'an and the Sunnah of the Prophet. He also said that the minorities in Pakistan would have no fear in an Islamic state since they would be treated in a just and a generous way.[320] That he was visualising Pakistan to be a caliphal state is also clear when he said that although one could not expect Pakistan to become a state of the *Khilafah al-Rashidah* overnight, the creation of Pakistan would certainly mean that it had taken the first step towards that. He envisioned that it would be on its way toward becoming truly an Islamic state established on the principles of the Qur'an.[321]

When confronted with questions such as how Pakistan could become a state like what he envisioned, when its leaders did not appear to be Islamic in their daily outward practice of Islamic rituals and like, Usmani would reply by saying that the *'ulama* had a responsibility to make such a

---

[318] See M. A. Al-Hasan, *Tajalliyate Usmani,* pp. 643-665.

[319] Although Usmani did not put it into explicit words, his implication was clearly to see Pakistan as a Caliphal State.

[320] Shabbir Ahmad Usmani, *Pegham,* p. 70-72.

[321] *Pegham,* p. 72.

state happen. Usmani said that the 'ulama should not let the future government of Pakistan fall into the hands of those who were not practicing Islam. If this were to happen, the *'ulama* would have only themselves to blame. One way to make sure this would not come to pass was for the *'ulama* to join the pro-league camp and to support it.

To the leaders he would frequently recall the responsibilities of an Islamic state. Usmani would quote the Qur'an and say, ". . . In the Qur'an, Allah says '[They are] those who, if we established them in the land, establish regular prayer, and give the Zakat, enjoin right and forbid wrong. With Allah rests the end (and decision) of (all) affairs. '"[322] He advised strongly never to enact any law in a future Pakistan that would be against the Islamic Shari'a.

(c) ABU 'L A'ALA MAWDUDI

Another *'Alim*, who helped Jinnah not because he (Mawdudi) joined the League, but because he turned away from the Congress, Was Abu `I A`ala Mawdudi.

Mawdudi was a pro-Khilafat participant who did not share the views of Madani on *muttahida qawmiyyah* (the single nation theory). In this regard, he developed serious differences with Madani. But although he did not agree with Madani on the single nation theory, it is interesting that he also rejected the League's proposal to create a separate nation for Muslims. Mawdudi regarded such a move to be contrary to Islam.[323] He equally rejected Indian nationalism because he said Hindus

---

[322] See Rizwan Malik, p. 198.

[323] Mawdudi regarded this as contrary to Islam because it would tantamount to 'nationalismt and would mean worship of a nation instead of worship of One Allah. This would be regarded as *shirk* (i.e., ascribing partners to Allah), a major sin in Islam. See Abul A'la Mawdudi, *Nationalism and India*, p. 45.

and Muslims did not form one nation.[324] Mawdudi wanted to create instead a universal state in India in which there was no prejudice of any kind against anyone and a socially Just state in which all citizens had full rights and full opportunities. He said this was not achievable under the concept of nationalism presented by the Congress and was surprised that some *'ulama* could not see this and were supporting the Congress. He said if Congress was to succeed, there would always be the difference between *qawm* and *ghayr qawm*. [325] He continuously held this view. His views became even stronger after the 1937 provincial elections in which Congress gained power. Mawdudi was disappointed at the way the Congress dealt with Muslims during their provincial rule in 1937-39. In his *Tahrik-i Azad-i Hind aur Musalman* he expressed his opinion by saying that he noticed the balance between the Congress and Muslims appeared as if it was between the ruler and the ruled. Mawdudi said that this spectacle was unbearable for him, as he felt distressed and very worried about the fate of Muslims in a future India.[326]

Mawdudi thought that if Muslims were to support Congress it would mean that they would turn away from their Muslim-ness because they would have to obey a non-Islamic congress. He said that the word "*qawm*" used by some congressmen was not used in a theological sense. It meant only "nation" or "nationality"[327]

Mawdudi began to express his political thinking more openly after 1937. As an editor of Tarjuman al-Qur'an, he expressed

---

[324] Initially, Mawdudi had supported Gandhi in his noncooperation movement. After Gandhi's falling out with the Khilafat movement and the communal violence that followed the collapse of the Khilafat movement, Mawdudi concluded that Hindus and Muslims cannot be considered to be one nation.

[325] See Abul A'ala Mawdudi, *Tehrik-i Azad-i Hind aur Musalman*, p. 299ff.

[326] Mawdudi, p. 300.

[327] See Rizwan Malik, pp. 340 ff.

his concerns about the future of Muslims in India.[328] He said that the only way to remove conflicts between Hindus and Muslims would be to revive genuine Islam[329] in opposition to the League's Lahore declaration of 1940 demanding separation from India, Mawdudi launched his own organisation. Mawdudi called it *Jama'at al-Islami* (the Islamic Community). One of the things this organization would do was to create a body of people who would engage themselves in extensive publication of Islamic literature, and in relief work and also propagation of Islam.

Mawdudi expressed most succinctly his views on what type of government Muslims should strive for in his *al-Jihad fi al-Islam*. In this work Mawdudi explains that unless there is a Divine government on the earth, man will rule with *fitna* (oppression) and *fasad* (injustice). Mawdudi took both these words from the Qur'an,[330] and explained that the government run with *fitna* and *fasad* has a particular trend. Such a government would be unscrupulous when it came to their interests because it would not be God-fearing. Since the

---

[328] Interestingly, Hindus became aware of their past civilisation as a result of Western learning and development of their self-identity. As a result of this, they began reviving their traditions but at the same time they began devaluing the Islamic cultural institutions they had become used to during the Islamic rule in India. Thus when Hindu nationalism began taking shape, as a result of the above, they could not break beyond the orbit of their religion. To Hindus 'nationalism' meant 'Hinduism'. See N. Ahmad, *Muslim Separatism in British India: A Retrospective Study,* p.77.

[329] BY this expression, it is possible Mawdudi meant his own party, the *Jama'at-i-Islami*. This is seen in collection of his works as an editor of *Tarjuman al-Qur'an* collected in three volumes and entitled *Muslaman aur Mawjudah Siyasi Kashmakash*. In it he warns Muslims of their annihilation in a Hindu majority if they believe in nationalism. Instead, the alternative he gave was to join the purely Islamic party, which he believed to be his own. See Malik, p. 211.

[330] See Qur'an, Ch 8:73.

basic purpose of any government is to be just and equitable, merely its coming into being is in itself unjust. Through such government evil will not be confined in one particular area but it will be like a fountainhead of many evils because its source is *fitna* and *fasad*. It will pose obstacles in the way of righteousness and will create agencies where the wrongdoers will find ways to carry out their deeds. Moreover, it will be seen that such governments will enact laws that will corrupt morals and will create factions among men. In brief, Mawdudi said that such governments will be agents to establish all kinds of evil on the earth and will also perpetuate those evils.

The remedy he proposed was a true struggle on the part of those who are righteous and understand this. The *jihad* that the righteous engage in may in the end require them even to wage a war until the government is replaced by the just and equitable government founded upon the fear of Allah and the Law He has ordained. This type of government will serve humanity and its purpose will be to see that righteousness flourishes and evil is obliterated. The purpose of its followers will be *Amr bi al-Ma 'ruf* and *Nahi 'an al-Munkar* (enjoining good and forbidding evil). [331]

As far as the issue of Pakistan itself was concerned, Mawdudi was worried about its potential government. He indicated that he would support the creation of Pakistan if it

---

[331] Note that everything that Mawdudi wrote in his is what Imam al-Husayn said when he gave his reasons for rising against Yazid (at the request of Muslims in Kufa who saw in Yazid's rule oppression and injustice). It is interesting also that Muslims in Kufa who invited Imam al-Husayn were worried on the issue of the institution of the Caliphate being in the hands of Yazid and wanted the Caliphate to revert to al-Husayn who they believed would return it to the Divine government of Allah. See Charles J. Adams translated passages of *al-Jihad fi al-Islam* in Aziz Ahmad and G.E. von Gruenbaum, *Muslim Self Statement in India and Pakistan*, pp. 155-158.

would be governed based on the concept of sovereignty of God and His Law.[332]

When it was settled in 1947 that India would be separated into two states, India and Pakistan, Mawdudi encouraged his party to vote for the League. He understood Pakistan would, after all, replace the individual Caliph with what he termed a "democratic Khilafat". Mawdudi hoped that it would be founded on the guidance vouchsafed to Muslims through the Prophet and might not only prove a blessing to the inhabitants of Pakistan but might encompass the whole world.[333]

With this kind of exposition coming from Mawdudi, and the other influential 'ulama clearly turning to his side, Jinnah could expect a massive tide of Muslim support.

There was one more issue that had already touched the hearts of a majority of Indian Muslims toward supporting an Islamic state of Pakistan. This was the Muharram issue. Although it is commemorated mainly by the Shi'as, many Sunni Muslims in India even today join the Shi'as in observing the Muharram days. It was mainly during the `Ashura[334]

---

[332] See Asim Nu'mani, *Makatib-i Sayyid Abul A'la Mawdudi*, Vol.2, pp.5ff.

[333] See Samat Sawlat, *Mawlana Mawdudi ki Taqariren*, p. 210. Also, Asim Nu'mani, *Rasail wa Masail*, 2 : 75.

[334] `Ashura is the 10th day of the first month of the Islamic calendar. There are many legends about the past events and future prophecies in Islam surrounding the significance of this day. As for the events that have already occurred in history, it is believed Moses delivered the Bani Israel from the bondage of Pharaoh on this day. Also, the flood in the Noah's time occurred this day. Sources on the Prophet's biography tell us that when he made his *hijra* from Mecca to Medina, when he arrived it was the tenth ('Ashara) of Muharram and coincided with the Jewish *Yom Kippur*. As for the future events, it is believed that 'Isa ibn Maryam (Jesus) will return this day with the Imam Mahdi signifying the end of this

processions in the Muharram mourning, that many times Hindus insulted Muslims. We have already seen earlier that these incidents sparked communal riots.

The tenth of the month of Muharram is the day internationally observed, particularly by the Shi`a Muslims, commemorating the martyrdom of Imam al-Husayn, the grandson of the Prophet. The event occurred in the year 61 AH (680 CE). To understand why it is so significant and how it relates to the issue of the caliphate, a little bit of historical background I think is important.

After the election of Abu Bakr as the first Caliph in the history of Islam, a clear split emerged as a group from among the Muslims believed that the rightful successor to the Prophet should have been `Ali.[335] They based their judgement on various incidents that took place during the mission of the Prophet that would indicate the Prophet had desired `Ali to be his successor.[336] Since this did not happen, the group who

_____

world as we know it. While all Muslims believe in the coming of Imam Mahdi with `Isa ibn Maryam, Shi`as believe the Imam Mahdi is their twelfth Imam, from the progeny of the Prophet, bearing the Prophet's name, now in occultation. The function of the Imam Mahdi and Jesus will be to establish the true caliphate on this earth that will bring the Kingdom of God with total social justice.

[335] `Ali ibn Abi Talib was the son-in-law of the Prophet and also his cousin. From among the youth he was the first one to have believed in the Prophet. `A l i remained faithful to the cause of Islam and participated with the Prophet in all his endeavor to establish Islam

[336] Among several incidents one that is often quoted is the event of *Ghadir al-Khum* near Makka. At this place the Prophet had asked the returning pilgrims to stop as he had an important message to deliver. As the pilgrims halted, the Prophet climbed a quickly erected pulpit and announced among other things that he would soon have to depart from this world but he was leaving behind two things which Muslims must hold on to if they were to attain

believed that 'Ali is the only one who should have become the Caliph clearly f e l t that 'Ali's rights were usurped. They also felt that the injunctions of the Prophet were violated.

When 'Ali did become the Caliph in 656 CE, three Caliphs (Abu Bakr, Umar and Uthman) had already preceded him. 'Ali s Caliphate lasted only six years, at the end of which he was assassinated by one of his enemies as he was praying in the early hours of the morning. The Caliphate passed to his son, al-Hasan but this was short-lived since circumstances had forced al-Hasan to sign a peace treaty with Mu'awiya (who was already a governor in Syria and had refused to give his allegiance both to 'Ali as well as to al-Hasan). With the peace treaty signed, Mu'awiya went on to establish the Umayyad dynasty that would l a s t to 750 CE at the end of which the

---

salvation. These were the Book of Allah (The Qur'an) and his Ahl al-Bayt (his immediate family). Then he lifted 'Ali by his side and lifting his hand he showed him to all and he gave a comprehensive sermon in which, referring to Ali, he also said, *Man kuntu nawla-hu fa hadha `Aliyyun Mawlahu* (Of whomever I am the Master, this `Ali is also his Master), and *Allahumma wali* man *walahu wa 'adi man a`dahu* (O Allah, be a friend of one who is his friend and be the enemy of the one who is his enemy). This incident is reported in major Sunni as well as Shi'a sources, The authenticity of this event is not questioned. What is questioned is the interpretation of the word "Mawla" in the text. The word *Mawla* comes from the Arabic word *Wali*, and besides meaning a "leader", it also means a "friend", a "patron", "Master". The Shi`as take this and several other incidents that occurred to claim the Prophet s injunction was for 'Ali to be his successor. While Sunnis do not dispute the event of the *Ghadir* and indeed other incidents, they insist that by the word "Mawla" the Prophet only meant perhaps "next of kin" or a "friend" or a Confidant. See S.H.M. Jafri, *The Origins and Early Development of Shia Islam* (London: Longman, 1979), pp. 19ff.

reins of caliphate would pass to the `Abbasids.[337]At the death of Mu'awiya, the Caliphate passed on to his son, Yazid.

It was in the time of Yazid that Karbala's `Ashura* day tragedy took place. As per the peace treaty al-Hasan had signed with Mu'awiya, the Caliphate should have gone to al-Hasan if he were alive but he had died before Mu`wiya.[338] Yazid was not considered by his subjects to be a rightful caliph. The image he portrayed was not perceived by his subjects as truly Islamic. They therefore wrote several letters inviting al-Husayn (the brother of al-Hasan) to save Islam and accept their wish and restore the Caliphate to himself as the rightful successor. After several requests, as the sources show, al-Husayn decided to find out the situation for himself. He sent for intelligence gathering information, while leaving his home town Madina with his family and friends to proceed towards

---

[337] The `Abbasids came to power as a result of the revolution staged by the Abbasids. It is very interesting to note that the reason why `Abbasids were successful in this revolution was the massive support from the public who thought the Umayyad's were unjust. The cry of the revolution was to avenge the martyrdom of Imam al-Husayn. The `Abbasids carried with them a black flag as a sign of mourning the martyrdom of Imam al-Husayn.

[338] We are told that al-Hasan was poisoned by Mu'awiya. It is shown that Mu'awiya promised al-Hasan's wife, a woman named Ju'da bint al-Ash'ath al-Qays, to marry her to his son Yazid provided that she poisoned al-Hasan. He also sent her a hundred thousand dirhams. She poisoned al-Hasan but Mu'awiya refused to marry her to his son Yazid saying that i f she could poison her husband al-Hasan there were no guarantees she would not do the same to his son Yazid. Instead, he married her to another person from the Banu-Talha as a substitute. The children she bore from this wedlock were reviled by the clan of Quraysh by referring to them as the "sons of a woman who poisons her husband". As al-Hasan lay on his death-bed he transferred his rights to succeed Mu'awiya to his brother al-Husayn. See Shaykh al-Mufid, *Kitab al-Irshad* p. 287. See also Peemahomed Ebrahim Trust, *Biography of Imam Hasan,* p. 52.

Kufa, from where he had received several requests. On the way he was intercepted at the place called Nainava (present day Karbala near Baghdad) by the forces of Yazid and brutally put to death with male members of his family, including his six-month-old son. As a grandson of the Prophet and beloved son of 'Ali and the Prophet's daughter Fatima, al-Husayn was held in high esteem by Muslims. The news of the tragic event sent shock waves through the world of Islam. This incident has since then been portrayed as a battle between the evil (Yazid) and the good (al-Husayn, the grandson of the Prophet). subjects to be a rightful caliph.

This was a turning point in the history of Islam. The Umayyad dynasty was never at peace after this and the Abbasid revolution in 750CE that toppled them had its inspiration in the Karbala event. Indeed Karbala's 'Ashura tragedy also took place on 'Ashura and at issue was the question of the caliphate and social justice. I find it interesting therefore that Indian Muslims were finding Karbala's 'Ashura tragedy inspiring. Although the Grand National Assembly in Turkey had abolished the seat of the Caliph in their hands, the institution of Caliphate itself, could still be revived. Through the process of *ijtihad*, the one-man Caliph could be substituted to a socially evolved democratic state.

With this brief background, we see that in twentieth-century India, Indian Muslims, Shi'a as well as Sunni, were again invoking Karbala's 'Ashura tragedy to arouse the passion of Muslims into siding with what they believed to be the injustices heaped upon them by the British government as well as the Hindus. The Khilafat movement had collapsed. The institution of the Caliphate was abolished, but all was still not lost. The glory that Islam had was when the Caliphate was intact could still be reestablished, now in the form of an Islamic state. Everything was in place: the party platform (All India Muslim League), and the effective leader (Muhammad Ali Jinnah), who was a modernizing nationalist and who seemingly had understood Iqbal's message in his Allahabad address. The only thing lacking, it seemed, was a massive theological support of the kind that was seen in the time of the Khilafat Movement. This appears to have been provided by the Karbala event, as follows.

In India, the Hindus and the British had become analogous to Yazid (in Urdu, *Yazidiyyat*, the force of evil and corruption). Muslims were analogous to the force of al-Husayn (in Urdu, *Husayniyyat*, force of the righteous, the one who had the right to the Caliphate so that he could establish a Divine government). The opportunity to arouse feelings of passion against the Hindus and the British could not be more perfect, as the previous Khilafatist leader Muhammad Ali, and also Iqbal and other thinkers like Josh Maliabadi began composing satirical poems using Karbala's `Ashura* tragedy to arouse theologically the passions of Indian Muslims. Gopi Chand Narang has collected selected poems in his book, *Saakhe-i-Karbala beturr-i-Sci 'iri Isti`ra: Urdu Shairi ek Takhliqi Rujhan,* from the Mughal period in India (16th century) down to our times until India received its independence from the British Raj (20th century). Narang divides the work of poets into four clear periods:

1. the Mughal period;

2. The period during the British Raj (particularly during and after the Balkan wars leading to the defeat of the Ottomans during the First World War and eventual partition of Islamic lands that belonged to the Ottoman empire and the eventual abolition of the Caliphate in Turkey) ;

3. the period after the collapse of the Khilafat movement in India as Muslims were struggling to find their place in India (particularly during and after the Congress rule in 1937); and finally the modern period after India's independence and the separation of Pakistan.

We observe that whenever people felt there were injustices committed in the land by the more powerful, the poets invoked people's emotions to right the wrong, using the Karbala event. In the Mughal period, the injustices committed were by the feudal lords. During the colonial period, the author perceives injustices committed were by the British government.[339]

The significance I see in this is when we have Khilafatist leaders like Muhammad Ali composing a poem invoking the Karbala event, his complaint is not only against the British government. At the time when he composed the poem, Khilafat movement had already petered out. Muslims saw themselves in a depressed state as they were struggling to have some political recognition in the areas of their majority in India. They considered themselves Mazlum (unjustly oppressed when they were in the right) much the same way as Muslims had become under Yazid when Karbala's `Ashura tragedy took place. It is worth noting that Imam al-Husayn's journey towards Kufa was to restore the rightful Caliphate and a just Islamic state.

Urdu publications show Muhammad Ali composing a poem that is clearly meant to arouse the emotions of Muslims who had clearly become despondent after the collapse of the Khilafat movement and the abolition of the Caliphate by the Grand National Assembly in Turkey. Moreover, the communal violence in India that was erupting even during the `Ashura procession to commemorate Karbala's `Ashura tragedy could be effectively used in a poem to arouse Muslims. Muhammad Ali composed a poem from the British prison in India:

> (0 Muslims!) the killing of al-Husayn (in Karbala) was in fact the death of Yazid (because) Islam (since then will forever) arise with a new life after every Karbala?'[340]

---

[339] Gopi Chad Narang, *Waak'e-i-Karbala beturr-i-Sci 'ri Isti'arra:Urdu Shairi ek Takhliqi Rujhan*, pp.11-44

[340] Narang, p. 28.

Qatl-e-Husayn 'asl me mar-ge Yezid hai
Islam zinda hota hai har Karbala ke ba'ad

Muhammad 'Ali's intentions are very clear. There is no need for Muslims to be despondent if the Khilafat movement has collapsed. There is no need to be despondent if the Caliphate has been abolished and usurped by the new "Yazids" of the modern times (that is, the Indian National Congress, or the Hindu majority in India or the National Assembly in Turkey). Islam will still revive itself after every calamity just as Karbala is alive (after the great sacrifice of Imam al-Husayn).

Iqbal in his earlier works had already composed a poem using Karbala's *'Ashura* tragedy and giving it a title to mean that Karbala was the meaning of "Free Islam".[341] In another poem, Iqbal explains:

The ever-living (and unchanging) truth is the status of Shabbir (another endeared name of Imam al-Husayn) While the colours of Kufis and Shaamis (tyrants of this world) keep changing.

Haqiqat-e abadi hai maqam-e Shabbiri
Badal t-e rehte hai andaazo Kufi-0 Shami [342]

Yet at another place Iqbal asks why is there no one in the caravan to follow the footsteps of al-Husayn, even though the waters of the (River) Euphrates[343] are still inviting.

---

[341] Ibid., pp. 34-37.

[342] Ibid., p. 34.

[343] In the event of Karbala, the River Euphrates stands as a very powerful symbol. Imam al-Husayn was intercepted and stopped at the banks of River Euphrates on the 2nd Muharram 61 AH. On the 7th Muharram the forces of Yazid compelled him to remove his tents away from the banks of the Euphrates. They also stopped the supply of water to his camps. On the 10th Muharram when they killed Imam al-Husayn and his male companions, they had

Iqbal's intentions do not appear to be any different than Muhammad Ali's. Iqbal uses more powerful images of Karbala in his poems and is appearing to be asking Muslims not to forget that Karbala was not just a historical event. It had its significance even in modern India.

Another poet in the same period was Josh Maliyabadi. Josh seems to have used Karbala's `Ashura tragedy to clearly show Muslims that they (Muslims) constituted a nation of their own. They had a duty to rise just as al-Husayn rose to march towards Kufa.

Oh the Nation! (referring to Indian Muslims and invoking them as a nation) Once again we have been plunged into the times of destruction. Islam seems to be again the target of the arrows (like al-Husayn who was the target of the arrows of Yazid at Karbala) of infidels.

Why are you so quiet?

Sing again with the same glory (and let the)
History record (again) the tales of men
Let Islam rise again, shining
Incumbent it is on each and every one to be' like Husayn Ibn Ali.

"*Ay Qawm*[344]*, wahi phir hai tabahi ka zamaana*
Islam hai phir tir-e hawadis ka nishana
Kyun chup hai? usi sham se phir ched tarana
Tarikh me reh jaayega mardon ka fasana
M i t-te huwe Islam ka naam phir jali-ho
Laazim hai har par ke Husayn ibn 'Ali ho[345]

---

not received any water for three days. The poet is alluding to this incident when he refers to the Euphrates.

[344] We have already seen that Sir Sayyid had used the word "Qawm" (nation) extensively in his writings and speeches even at the time when the word 'nationalism' was unknown anywhere.

[345] Narang, p. 36.

After the First World War, in response to the Rowlatt Act, Gandhi united his non-cooperation movement with the Indian Muslims Khilafat movement. At this time, there were Khilafat movement propagandists in Turkey. Material issued by them was proscribed. The tragedy of Jalianwalla Bagh in 1919 promoted anti-government poetry. After the collapse of the Khilafat movement, communal tensions were responsible for more poetry considered "seditious" by the British government. During this period, and shortly afterwards as the Pakistan movement was gathering momentum, poems invoking Karbala's `Ashura tragedy also appeared. These poems were in response to the Hindu attack upon Muslims during the `Ashura tragedy commemoration of Imam al-Husayn.

The poets have invoked the Karbala event, this time directly against Hindus who had been disrupting the Muharram procession of the `Ashura day. Thus, in a collection by several poets put together under the title *Yadgar-i Karbala: Bambai ka Khuni Muharram* (Memories of Karbala : Bombay's Bloody Muharram), we find very interesting poems where Muslims are passionately invoking Karbala's `Ashura tragedy to explain their plight and suffering under the Hindu majority. In a poem *Darbar-i Husayn men Musalmanon ki Faryad* (Complaints of Muslims in the Court Of Husayn) we read:

How unbearable (are the) events (that) are unfolding in Muharram
The land of the city (Bombay) is turning into Karbala
Muslims are enduring pain and suffering
The (rivers of) blood of the poor *Ummat* (Muslims) is flowing
From (the districts of) Barel and Dadar to Mahim
There is no resistance against the oppressors
It has reached to the end of oppression
They are creating this hell in Muharram
They are stopping supplies of food and water[346]

---

[346] The poet here is giving the parallel with the Karbala event. We have already seen that for three days before the day of `Ashura,

They are turning each street into Kufa[347]
They are re-enacting the signs (of 'Ashura) everywhere
The stores are shut and the market is quiet
The (Muslim) districts are collections of quiet

Muharram men kaisi jafaa ho rahi hal
Zamin shahar ki Karbala ho rahi hai
Musalman ranj-0-alam seh rahi hai
Ghariban m a t ki khun beh r hai
Barel or Dadar se le ta-be Mahim
Nahin hai koi zalim ke mazamin
Sitam ki ab inthiha ho rahi hai
Muharram me ye has& bapa kiya hai
Gharibon pe band abo dana kiya hai
Gali kuche Muslim pe Kufa kiya hai
Har ek jagha 'ibrat ki jaa ho rahi hai
Dukane hai pat or Baazar suney hai
Mohalle hai saehre khamoshi ke kuche

In the same poem, a little later, the poet is making a complain to the British government for having reduced the status of Muslims so low that Muslims are made to suffer.

We have a complaint against our Government
In your government this is our status (that)
The heaps of atrocities are laid down upon (us)
Upon us, (your) subjects, ate laid these troubles
The oppressors accuse us to be the guilty
And put us into the jails to suffer the hardships

---

the forces of Yazid had stopped the supply of water to al-Husaynls camp. See al-Mufid, p. 343.

[347] The poet here is referring to the streets of Kufa before where (the household of al-Husayn) were taken as the captives of Karbala in chains and humiliated beforfe proceeding to Sham (Damascus) in Syria.

Heme apni Sarkar se hai ye shikwa
Hukumat me teri hamara ye darja
Gharibon pe ahle sitam ka hai nargha
Raiyyat pe joro-jafa ho rahi hai
Hami-ko sitamghar mujrim banaye
Hami qayd-khanon ki sakhti uthaye

At one point, the poet is counting losses Muslims suffer, in spite of what the poet calls the *wafaa* (loyalty) of Muslims towards Hindus, and sarcastically blames Gandhi for this:

They looted our stores, set fire to mosques
Corpses upon corpses lay dead
Look! this is what is Gandhi's wish being fulfilled
If a Hindu strayed into the district of a Muslim
The Muslim would save the infidel against all calamities
(As for Muslims) not even their children returned alive.
Instead of loyalty, it is the disloyalty being portrayed

Dukano ko luta, Masajid jalay-i
Shahidon ki lashon pe lashen bichaai
Yeh Gandhi ki dekho Raza ho rahi hai
Muhalle me Muslim ke Hindu jo aaya
Har afat se Kafir shaki-ko bachaya
Musalmanon ka baccha bhi zinda na aaya
Wafaa ke b i l-i f a z jafaa ho rahi hai

In another collection entitled *Hindu lidaron-se Musalmanon ka Shikwa* (Complaints of Muslims' Against Hindu (Congress) Leaders), a poem from the proscribed material reads:

Muslims are giving this call (to the Hindu leaders)
0 you who call for the Independence (swarajya)
Where are you?
Only until yesterday Muslims and Hindus were
brothers unto each other
Whereas today they fight each other
How sad the world has come to be

It is said to a brother, you are a brother
Muslims are giving this call [to the Hindu leaders]

De rahe hain ye Muslim Duha-i
Aaj Swaraj walo, kahan ho
Hindu Muslim the kal Bhai-Bhai
Aaj hoti hay in me Lard-i
Kaysi afsos hai Jag hinsa-z
Kaha jata hai Bhai ko Bhai
De rahe hain ye Muslim Duha-i

We knew you would betray (us)
Pretending to console but you will take life
One day you will turn away from us
You will be with but still not with us
What a calamity has fallen upon us
Hindu soldiers shooting us with bullets
It did not help to be faultless
Help us! Help us! O Allah.

Ham samajhte the turn dhoke doge
Dam dilase-se turn jan loge
Balke ek din dagha hamko doge
Tum kisike huwe ho na hoge
Kaisi day-i hai ham par tabahi
Goliyan mare Hindu sipahi
Ram ayi na kuch be-gunahi
al-Madad, al-Madad, Ya Ilahi

In another poem, a poet is trying to raise the morale of Muslims again using the Karbala event:

We are the servants of the Shah of Karbala (al-Husayn)
We are fully aware of all kinds of oppression

Ham ghulam-i shahe Karbala hai
waqif-i zulmo joro jafa hal

Earlier on, Haji Ahmad had composed his strongest emotive poems he called "The Pain of Khilafat" (*Dard-i Khilafat*) in which he invoked Karbala symbols fully:

This Khilafat is a newly-wed who sacrificed
(just as) ibn Haider (Imam al-Husayn) became a martyr
for the sake of Allah
(when he) took Asghar[348] in his lap and said to Shimr[349]
I need a little water for the sake of my beloved
The devilish (Shimr) looked at Asghar saying
Why have you brought him here for the sake of dying
Saying here is the water for the sake of your descendent
Alas! slashed was the thirsty throat of Akbar[350]
(All these atrocities) for the sake of the Messenger
With the cup of martyrdom in his hands said al-Husayn
For Islam I will be a slaughter for the sake of Allah

---

[348] Nothing brings more passion in the days of Muharram than recalling the tragic incident in Karbala when Imam al-Husayn took his six-month-old son Ali Asghar in front of the army appealing to their conscience and showing them what the three-day thirst had done to his six-month old son. The savagery of the enemies reaches to its climax as they shoot an arrow at the neck of Ali Asghar. In the context of this poem, the poet is drawing the parallel of those who wanted to destroy the Caliphate to the forces of Yazid. It is important to note the issue at Karbala was also the issue of the Caliphate. Yazid was considered a usurper of the caliphate that Muslims believed belonged to Imam al-Husayn and they invited him to Kufa, promising him their support. See Appendix 9.

[349] Shimr is shown as the one who was bitterly against Imam al-Husayn and was instrumental in perpetrating all kinds of hostilities against Imam al-Husayn and his family.

[350] Akbar was another son of Imam al-Husayn in Karbala. War was still a youth and he too was killed in a manner that arouses passion and emotion at what Muslims believe were the savagery and deliberate plots against Islam. The unique thing in India was that both the Shi`as and Sunnis took part in re-creating these events. Muslim poets were fully aware of this. Most of them were Sunnis.

In another poem he again invokes Karbala symbols:

The residents of Kufa invited, then deceived
One who quenched thirst was himself slaughtered thirsty
No shame or remorse did you show 0 devilish Shimr
When you slaughtered the beloved son of Fatemah[351]
0 Shimr! What do you expect on the Day of Judgment
For little water you deprived and killed Asghar

In early 1920's, Haji Ahmad produced his collection of the strongest poems containing the Karbala symbols. The poet gave Karbala a clear parallel to the Khilafat movement since he called his composition, Dard-i Khilafat (The Pain of Khilafat). The Khilafat movement was still in progress. It is significant to note that the events of Karbala had already begun to appear even then :

Wuh Khilafat hai keh dolah tuk jis par huwa shahid
de diya sat ibn Haider ne Khuda ke waaste
Gowd-men Asghar ko hake Shah ye bole ay Shimr
Chaahiye thoraa sa pani dil-ruba ke waaste
Dekh kar Asghar ki jaanib yun laga kehne laeen
kyun laaye ho turn is ko kaza kc waaste—
Tir ek chora keh basu sheh gala Asghar chhida
Bola yeh pani hay lo al haya ke waaste
Haay Akbar ke gale pyaase pi? khanjar chal gaya
Gham uthaaye hain Mustafa kc waaste
Haath par jam i shahadat le kc Sarwar ne kaha
Din par katwaayenge sur hum Khuda ke waaste
Kufa walon ne yeh kiya bulwa kc Kufa men dagha
Saqi-i Kawsdr ko haay zfbah pyasa kar diya
Kcch na ghayrat hay tujhko ay Shimr-i Laeen
Fatemah ka ladla aur tune zibah kar diya

---

[351] Fatemah binti Muhamnmad. The poet is referring to the daughter of the Prophet Muhammad whose son al-Husayn was.

Kya milegi abr roz jaza tumko ay laeen
Ik zara se aab par Asghar ko kushta kar diya[352]

This appears to be the greatest help Jinnah received. Importantly, Jinnah himself was a Shi'a. Although he never invoked Karbala's `Ashura tragedy in his speeches or in his writings, he cannot have failed to understand it fully[353].

As a Shi'a himself, he also participated in Muharram programmes. Jinnah did not have to spell out anything that would jeopardise the future of Islam in the eyes of the British government. It was not his style. But one could clearly see that he used Islam to further the cause of the Pakistan movement

---

[352] See Haji Ahmad, *Dard-i Khilafat, Ya`ni Kalam-i Ahmad*, Proscribed Material, Entry number 1393. See also Titles 1400; 1401; 1403, published and proscribed by the British government in Lahore and in Punjab. These various collections were published both before and after the Khilafat movement. These tracts contain patriotic poems that demanded total freedom from the British government. These entries also include the famous Hymn from Iqbal which became part of the daily assembly in schools. Until partition this famous hymn of Iqbal, saare jahan se atcha hai watan hamara, was sung as part of the daily assembley hymn. These tracts also include poems from Syed A l i Hussain Shah A l i and others making strong plea for the Hindu-Muslim unity during the non-co-operation period, 1919-1922, for the sake of India's freedom.

[353] Although there are no direct references available to my knowledge where Jinnah has invoked in his speeches and writings the Karbala event, there are oral accounts where Jinnah has referred to the Karbala event. In one incident when he was officially invited by the Viceroy to India to attend a function in honour of the King, J i ~ a h is said to have turned down the invitation. Interestingly, the oral tradition says that the reason he gave for not attending the function was that it happened to be the `Ashura day and therefore he would be mourning on that day for the "King of all the other kings, Imam al-Husayn `Alayhi-Salam'.

to his fullest advantage. Echoing Iqbal's Allahabad address of 1930, he said on different occasions that

> Muslims constituted a nation of their own "with our own distinctive culture and civilisation, language and literature, art and architecture . . . sense of values and proportions, legal laws and moral codes"[354], systems and calendar, history and traditions, aptitudes and ambitions—in short, we have our own distinctive outlook on life and of life. By all canons of international law, we are a nation.[355]

Jinnah believed, as he said, that Islam regulated everything in a Muslim's life. It regulated things from one's ceremonies to one's daily life, from the salvation of the soul to the health of the body, from the punishments in this world to the punishments in the life hereafter. It was a complete code that regulated every department of life, whether individually or collectively.

After Jinnah's three-pronged approach to win the majority of Muslims to the League, there was no turning back for Muslims. Apart from the few *'ulama* who remained loyal to the Congress, almost all other *'ulama* came out openly supporting the League.[356] Their message to Muslims was simple and very appealing to the majority of Indian Muslims. They reminded

---

[354] See http://www.scribd.com/doc/102239725/5/,"The Ideology of Pakistan". See also www.rebuildpakistan.net and "Quaid e Azam Mohammad Ali Jinnah", in http://az-mohaljinnah.blogspot.com/

[355] Pirzada, *Quaid-Azam Jinnah's Coprrespondence*. See also High Commission For Islamic Republic of Pakistan New Delhi, http://pahic-newdelhi.blogspot.com.

[356] Towards the end, the *'ulama* who advocated a "one nation theory" found themselves more and more alienated from their own followers. Thus, we are told, that even Husain Ahmad Madanifs theory *"muttahida qawmiyyah"* was not palatable even to his own followers and when he stood up to speak about it only a few hundred from a gathering of ten thousand would be prepared to

Muslims that they will be answerable to Allah on the Day of Judgment. This, they said, cannot be avoided. They appealed Muslims to vote with their conscious.[357]

The Muslim women too came out fully supporting the League. They found great appeal in Karbala's `Ashura tragedy because it was the sister of Al-Husayn, Zaynab bint `Ali, who brought to light the misdeeds of Yezid and the atrocities his forces committed against al-Husayn. Zaynab remained a model for women because of her sacrifices in Karbala and afterwards as the prisoner in Yezid's court.

On the political front, what also helped Jinnah was the fact that the British government was witnessing the devolution of its authority in India. This manifested itself at two levels: first, the declining authority of the British government as it was facing several Indian movements prior to the Second World War; and second, the impending Hindu rule after the departure of the British.

The East India Company solidified its hold over India in the name of the British monarch. After the 1857 uprisings, the British government took over the full control of India from the hands of the East India Company. [358]British government

---

listen to him. See K.K. Aziz, *The Making of Pakistan: A Study in Nationalism,* p. 181.

[357] See Shabbir Ahmed Usmani, *Khutba t-i-Sadara t Meeru t Muslim League*, p. 11.

[358] It was by no means an easy transition. In the first half of the nineteenth century, there were spontaneous uprisings as the various Indian tribes with their chiefs protested against the East India Company's colonising practices. There were uprisings in Delhi region as Indians took up arms against the British rulers. There were uprisings also from feudal lords who protested in 1817-1818 against the introduction of taxation on rent-free service lands. Similar uprisings were witnessed between 1826-1829 in Poona district. There were peasant uprisings in Bombay Presidency

was very concerned that uprisings of the kind that occurred in 1857 should not occur again. In order for them to hold on to India as their possession, they not only used military force but also created strong and efficient bureaucracy to maintain law and order.[359]They enacted several acts and regulations in this regard.[360] These ranged from the time they wanted to keep what they called "the "saturnalia of lawlessness"[361] emanating from Bengal to the Defence Act of 1915 to the notorious Rowlatt Act 1919. After the Rowlatt Act and the Jalianwalla Bag massacre that followed in 1919 the British government adopted the policy of patient restraint during the Khilafat and Non-cooperation movements.

The British government took strict measures again during the civil disobedience actions in late 1920's and early 1930's [362] including collective fines and harsh punishments. When the "Quit India" movement began in 1942, the British government

---

between 1821-1831. There were revolts by Orissians in 1845 and in 1855, the great Santhal revolt took place in the Santhal Parganas. See Jagamath Sarkar, A. B. Bardhan and N. E. Balram, *India's Freedom Struggle: Several Streams*, pp. iii-xiii.

[359] See Hayat, p. 81.

[360] Michael O'Dwyer, *India as I Know It, 1885-1925,* p. 298.

[361] Hayat, p. 81.

[362] Several organised sectors of Indian workers had arisen in the late 1920's and 1930's as part civil disobedience action. There were uprisings against *Zamindars* and peasants in the Uttar Pradesh. In one army unit, even a section of the army unit revolted to join the civil disobedience at the Gahnval unit. In defiance of a ban imposed by the British government against demonstrations, more than 30,000 workers had come out to demonstrate on the streets of Bombay against the arrival of the Simon Commission. Gandhi had moved a resolution during the Lahore Congress Session in 1930 for a Civil Disobedience for complete independence. Gandhi remained unsupportive for these movements when he saw that these sectors were supporting violence. See Sarkar, pp. 30 ff.

pursued it with severe punishment.[363] Some politicians likened their rule to "the police conception of a state"[364]

Indian Muslims had not forgotten the promises the British government had given Muslims in India in the in the last war. Nevertheless, the second world war changed the whole situation in India. The British government was seen as exhausted and broken. They were faced with enormous problems of afterward reconstruction. They became keen to pull resources out of India, not put them into it.[365] If they continued their hold on India, the British taxpayer would have suffered. The British government had enacted several acts designed to bring about reform in their rule in India. The last such Act was in 1935; but although intended to provide reform to the British rule, the Act made the British Parliament supreme over Indian affairs in several respects.[366] Jinnah called it ninety-eight percent safeguards and two percent authority. Indians were interested in the power at the centre.

---

[363] When Gandhi proclaimed in August of 1942 his famous "Quit India" slogan, the British government took heavy-handed measures against National leaders by rounding them up and imposing strict punishments against Indians. Spontaneous strikes broke out as a result of this measures with more left-wing groups like the Communist Party calling upon its supporters to observe "antirepression day". Urgent demands were made for the release of the national leaders who were rounded up and jailed. Some groups even called for the formation of a "national government for national defence". See Sarkar, p. 111.

[364] *Jawaharlal Nehru: An Autobiography,* p. 435.

[365] Hayat, p. 84 ff.

[366] At least in three respects, the Act of 1935 made the British Parliament supreme over Indian affairs. These included the "diarchy" at the centre which gave the Governor-General powers over defence and foreign affairs. Second, all safeguards in the constitution were placed in the hands of the Governor-General; and third, the federation would be subservient to the British Parliament. See Hayat, p. 86.

With the Second World War and its pressures upon the British government, there was a definite devolution in British authority over its Indian subjects. The prospects for Indians to get power at the centre increased with the devolution in British authority. At the same time, the fear of Muslims in India also increased and it became apparent to them that with the end of British rule in India, it would have to be replaced by Hindu rule. This power, based on democracy, would mean that Muslims would forever be in the minority and therefore subservient to Hindus.

The Muslims did not have a happy experience during the Congress rule dominated by Hindu parliamentarians in the Provinces in 1937-1939. This definitely turned many Muslims against them, as they clearly felt that the system was biased against them and was favouring the Hindus as the majority. The British government realized that the democratic system was not suitable for India because it did not contain population of homogeneous stock. There was a flaw in the system as far as India was concerned because by applying principles of democracy in India, it (democracy) left Muslims the "permanent" minority with no chance ever to turn them into majority situation. Muslims began to fear that the devolution in British authority was working against their vital interests.[367]

---

[367] It is to be noted that there are sharp divisions among scholars of Indian history as regards to Muslims' demand for Pakistan. The idea of a Muslim separate state, apart from continuous opposition from some notable *'ulama* like Shaykh Mahmud al-Hasan Madani and Abul Kalam Azad, deeply troubled Hindus as well as the British. To the Hindus, territorial unity of India formed part of their deeply held beliefs. To the British, undoing what they believed to be "politically united" India would be something unacceptable. Scholars, therefore, have examined these issues with great debate. The recent of such argument is from Ayesha Jalal in her *The Sole Spokesman: Jinnah, th e Muslim League and the "Demand for Pakistan."* In her book, Ayesha Jalal argues that Pakistan failed to satisfy the interests of the very Muslims who are supposed to have

As a result of the massive support from all sectors of Indian Muslims, the League won a landslide victory. This led to the formation of Pakistan, an Islamic State that was supposed to function in place of the Caliph, the vicegerent of Allah on the earth.

The first lines of the Constitution of Pakistan attest to the fact that it was created so that Muslims in it would uphold the laws of Allah and enjoin good on the mankind and forbid evil.

---

demanded its creation. She is wondering how a Pakistan came about which so poorly fitted the interests of most of its people. Taking the Lahore Resolution of 1940 as her focus, Ayesha Jalal argues that the demand for Pakistan was dictated by the British needs. The Congress were demanding independence and the constituent assembley. To counterweigh this demand, the Viceroy Linlithgow asked Jinnah to present All India Muslim League's constructive policy. For this purpose, Ayesha Jalal states that Jinnah was the best guarantee the British government could find against a united political demand. See pp. 40ff.

CHAPTER FIVE:
CONCLUSIONS

Although the Khilafat movement collapsed, the evidence we have seen in this thesis suggests that it was not a totally failed attempt. As a movement struggling for freedom from western domination, the Khilafat movement itself was not a unique phenomenon.

There were many other movements elsewhere in the world at the time of the Khilafat movement in India. They were either struggling against Western domination or struggling for their own nationalist cause. We find therefore anti-Western movements in Russia and China in the years 1919-1925; or the nationalist movements like the Afghan War of 1919, the Egyptian revolt of 1919, the hostilities within the Ottoman empire in 1919-1925 and even in Iran, the Persian nationalist movements of 1919-1925.[368]

What is unique about the Khilafat movement is that it was a movement in which we find combined ingredients of both nationalism and pan-Islamism. The Khilafat movement was not an entirely nationalist movement against the Western domination of India. It was a movement that was largely inspired for theological reasons. It was not entirely a nationalist movement because it had a pan-Islamist ingredient in it and therefore, its ideal extended to include all Muslims everywhere.

---

[368] See J. Kennedy, *Asian Nationalism in Twentieth Century*, pp. 83f f. See also A. J. Toynbee, "Relation between British India, Soviet Russia and Afghanistan, 1919-1923" in Survey of International Affairs 1920-1923, pp.1-2.

In that sense, the Khilafat movement extended beyond India's boundaries to include the whole community of not only the majority Sunni Muslims. Shi`a Muslims had always supported the pan-Islamist ideals but the Khilafat movement, invoked the deepest sentiments of Shi`a Muslims as the Khilafatist leaders used the examples of the martyrs of Kerbala in their appeal to win support of all Muslims. It was nationalist only in the sense that between the years 1919 and 1923 it supported the predominantly Hindu non-cooperation movement led by Gandhi. It can also be argued, however, that the main reason Muslims joined Gandhi vs. non-cooperation movement was the British policy towards Turkey and the Caliphate.

Even if followers of the Khilafat movement were using pan-Islamic symbols to create for themselves some kind of reconciliation with their Indian nationality and their pan-Islamic identity, it was still not entirely unique in this sense because other Islamic countries had similar movements in place at that time.[369]

Some scholars have suggested that the Khilafat Movement was primarily a campaign by a particular group of Indian Muslim leaders whose purpose was to unite Muslims using religious and cultural symbols meaningful to all Muslims. Therefore, it is suggested, it was a quest for a "pan-Indian Islam". If they were able to unite themselves to form a pan-Indian Muslim constituency they would have a true opportunity to participate in the Indian nationalist movement. The reasoning behind such a move was to offset their minority status by being able to bargain either with the Hindus or the British from the position of strength and thus to acquire political concession.[370] On the surface, this seemed like an impossible task given the vast regional, linguistic, and sectarian diversity among Indian Muslims.

---

[369] The problem for Indian Muslims was unique in the sense that it was still a minority in pre dominantly Hindu society.

[370] See Minault, pp. 2-3.

There was one common denominator, however, that could overcome all these hurdles. This common denominator was a shared sense of loyalty to Islam and its Five Pillars, which gave Muslims homogeneity even if they differed in other respects. This could be used to unite them and mobilise them. This thesis has shown that it was this denominator that had galvanised all Muslims both during the Khilafat movement and later during the Pakistan movement. The Proscribed Material has shown us that poets and writers invoked Muslims through this factor. And indeed this was the factor, as Minault has suggested, that was utilised by Indian Muslims to forge the Indian Muslims' own political constituency.[371]

Interestingly, however, when Hindus and Muslims united together in Gandhi's non-cooperation movement in 1920, an important leader from the 'ulama, Maulana Mahmud al-Hasan, gave the reasons for Muslims joining the agitations. It was not because of any attachment to nationalism or Gandhi's noncooperation movement. It is strange, but he even indicated that it was not even because Muslims were strongly protesting the British domination. Their sole reason for joining the agitations was that the holy places in Mecca and Medina were being exploited in favour of the Sharif of Mecca. Maulana Mahmud al-Hasan said that if the British government could take steps to convince the Muslims that the Sharif of Mecca would make peace with the Ottoman Caliph, that he would personally intervene and make sure that Muslims withdraw from all agitation against the British government not only in India but also across the frontier.[372]

It is also true that the issue of the Caliphate was affecting only the Muslim community. In itself, the issue of the Caliphate was of no interest or concern to the Hindus, except that it offered an opportunity for friendship and the brotherhood

---

[371] Minault, pp. 2-3.

[372] See A.C. Niemeijer, *The Khilafat Movement in India, 1919-1924*, The Hague, 1972, pp. I 62 ff.

slogan "*Hindu Muslim Bhay Bhay*". Gandhi explained his feelings clearly in one of the letters he wrote to the Viceroy, dated 22 June 1920, in which he said,

"I consider that as a staunch Hindu wishing to live on terms of the closest friendship with any of my Mussalman countrymen, I should be an unworthy son of India if I did not stand by them in their hour of trial".[373]

It is clear from this that apart from an opportunity it provided to cement the Hindu-Muslim relations, the caliphate itself meant nothing to Gandhi or other Hindu leader.[374] It seems that both Hindus and Muslims realised the irreconcilable nature of their existence. Both realised, it seems, that their nationalism can only be true if it is tied up with their own religious communities. Each community had their own ideology which emphasised their social, economical and political unit, strongly bound to their religion. Deviation from this just did not happen.[375] This explains why Muslims did not take up the cause of independence with Hindus for a united India in spite of the fact that they were Indians too. Muslims seem to have been asking themselves about the end result of all this. If India was to free itself from the British rule, that would only be replaced by Hindu rule. With this fear in their mind, their alliance with the Hindus was always cautious and conditional. We saw this in the Lucknow pact of 1916, when the future rights of both

---

[373] See Niemeijer, p. 169. See also Full text of "Speeches And Writings M.K.Gandhi", http://www.archive.org/stream/speechesand writi032213mbp/speechesandwriti032213mbp_djvu.txt

[374] The British observers always referred to the Hindu-Muslim unity as "artificial". See Niemeijer, p. 170.

[375] Apparently this was the general trend of thought in the British minds as well. There was about India an image that Indian society was primarily a conglomeration of disparate communities, races and tribes. See Farzana Shaikh, *Community and Consensus in Islam: Muslim Representation in Colonial India, 1860-1947 (Cambridge: Cambridge University Press, 1989)*, pp. 230-231.

communities were carefully stipulated. We saw that it broke down in 1928 with the Nehru Report, and distrust never left the Muslim side.[376]

In an interesting study by Farzana Shaikh,[377]we are told that the decline of Muslim power and the consolidation of British rule did not make Muslims resign to their fate. On the contrary Muslims renewed vigorously their efforts to restore the dignity of Islam. They were convinced that their salvation lay in returning to the fundamentals of the faith. But they differed on the course of their action to achieve this. In that sense then, we can clearly see that there were two different paths created by two different sets of 'ulama. Their goal was the same, the means to achieve this was different.

First, there were the "reformers". They regarded Islam as a religious and cultural entity. Their concern mainly lay in safeguarding Islam because they believed that if faith was safeguarded, the Muslim community would not disintegrated. They concluded that faith and integrity of Islam was to be safeguarded not by political action but by a process of cultural resistance. This had to be sustained by elaborate rules governing individual behaviour derived from the Shari'a. It is noteworthy that they never lost the vision that Islam was a polity and needed to be wielded. Their approach was to defend the cultural ideal because in doing so they believed

---

[376] Niemeijer, pp. 170 ff.

[377] Farzana Shaikh, *Community and Consensus in Islam: Muslim Representation in Colonial India, 1860-1947*, (Cambridge, Cambridge University Press, 1989)pp. 228ff. Farzana Shaikh argues in her book that politics of the period (particularly in the early twentieth century leading to the partition) cannot be explained by merely referring to the pragmatic interests. Islam has in its tradition influence of ideas. This is an important dimension in Islam which needs to be explained to show what determined a particular political experience.

that re-generation of the Islamic ideal would occur. There were efforts made to project this onto a national Indian culture.[378]

Then there were the *'ulama* who followed the path of Sir Sayyid. Their purpose was to restore the pre-eminence of the Indian Muslims in the hierarchy of power in modern times. They did not stress intensification of faith or withdrawal from communal affairs. Rather, they hoped to consolidate a distinct Muslim identity that would shape itself by the forces of modern, Western education.[379]

In a situation like this, Muslims were not altogether enemies of the British, even though Muslims sided with Gandhi between 1920 and 1923. We see this clearly in the attitude of the Agha Khan and Syed Ameer Ali and even the Ali brothers after 1930.

When scholars look at this divided loyalty they think that Muslims were going through some kind of identity crisis. Niemeijer says that "it was a movement of a group searching for its own identity and trying to assert it[380]. This identity crisis has also been referred to as a struggle the Indian Muslims were

---

[378] See David Lelyveld, *Aligarh's First Generation: Muslim Solidarity in British India* (Princeton: Princeton University Press, 1978), pp. 345ff. David Lelyveld shows us in his book that in following the line of Sir Sayyid, the politically active Muslims had believed and had vigorously pursued the argument that the individual's political preferences were always governed by his religious affiliations. Therefore, since Hindus formed the largest religious group, they would always be dominant over Muslims. Sir Sayyid had objected to the democracy where arithmetically one-man one-vote would certainly fail to take into account special claims made by Indian Muslims because their social and political importance in shaping India would not be reflected in their numbers. See also Shaikh, pp. 233-234.

[379] Shaikh, pp. 229 ff.

[380] Niemeijer, p. 167.

going through to create for themselves an Islamic world in which they could live as Indians.[381]

With the abolition of the Caliphate, this dissertation contends, Muslims were left helpless and despondent, but this did not turn them away from the concept of the Caliphate in which they so strongly believed. They remodelled their thought process so that the concept could fit in with the new situation they were in, in the twentieth century. A proper Islamic solution vis-à-vis the modern age was required. In a situation like this, as we have seen, Iqbal came up with an authentically Islamic solution. This was the principle of *ijtihad*.

There were still questions about how would one come to terms with the modern-day concept of nationalism. We have seen earlier that Muslims possessed divided loyalties. Even those *'ulama* who were championing "one-nation theory"[382] were not entirely convinced that Muslims would be able to achieve full equality under Hindu domination. Iqbal clarified this for Muslims when he said that nationalism to Islam meant people bound by ideology. 1f people were bound in race or language or the colour of their skin it would only mean another form of divisiveness.

With the theory in place and the masses already trained during the days of the Khilafat Movement, it was not difficult for Muhammad Ali Jinnah to come up with his three-pronged approach, which we have described, and to win Muslims of all shades to his side in his Pakistan movement.

But if Muslims in their massive support for Pakistan were analogous to brick in building an edifice called Pakistan, the foundation and the mortar to hold that edifice must have been

---

[381] See Niemeijer, p. 168. See also J. W. Watson, *Muhammad Ali and the Khilafat Movement*, p. 56.

[382] The two prominent *ulama* were Maulana Madani and Maulana Abul Kalam Azad.

the Karbala event. We have explored some dimensions of its significance in Chapter 4. We saw earlier that the method of communication for Muslims was all at a local level. That is to say, the communication took place by means of the vernacular press, *khutbas* in the mosques, pamphlets and handbills, composition and recitation of poetry, demonstrations and processions. Muharram processions on 'Ashura days accompanied by pamphlets, and hand-bills on which were printed poems about Karbala were enough to arouse the emotions of Muslims at the time when they were feeling hopeless about their future under Hindu rule.

It is appropriate now to provide some interpretation, or at least a hypothesis, concerning the thought process implied in Iqbal's theory. He certainly directed the Indian Muslims into modern and rational thinking, yet without deviating from the main Islamic principles. At the same time, this thinking helped Jinnah in his bid to win Muslims to his side in the Muslim League, then championing for a separate Islamic state.

Iqbal, in his many compositions, refers to the problem of *shirk* (ascribing partners to Allah) in Islam. In one of his classic compositions he creates an imagery of "the parliament of Satan" (Majlis-e-Iblis-e-Shura), in which he explains the evolution of modern societies to the point where societies have formed themselves into democratic states. Referring to those democracies in which the people as a majority make laws at the expense of Divine laws, where God is totally left out, Iqbal lets Satan's Members of Parliament explain such an institution in these words:

Hamne khud-ne pehnaya hai inko shahi libaas
Ab zara Adam huwa hai khud shinaso khud nigar

We have ourselves dressed people in kingly clothes
Now that a human being has evolved.

The evolution implied here is of a humankind that has moved in its thinking to accept institutions of democracy, i.e. popular sovereignty. In other words, Iqbal is saying that there is no difference between an aristocrat who rules like a Pharaoh (thinking himself to be the god) and the modem institutions of democracy where God is not regarded as the true Sovereign. In his thinking, this is the greatest shirk of modern times. It is the work of Iblis, who has only fooled mankind by clothing an aristocrat, in the garb of democracy so that now it is the population as a whole doing what was done by the aristocrat.

When this is converted to the theory of the institution of the Caliphate, we begin to see the impact of his theory on the minds of Indian Muslims who were genuinely interested in saving the Caliphate.

The Caliphate is the opposite of sovereignty. The Caliph is the vicegerent of God on the earth and his purpose in Islam is to establish the ordinances of God for a just society. Interestingly, this status was given to all mankind when God created the first human being on the earth. Historically, the direct Caliphs of God on earth were the prophets in all categories.[383] They were understood as receiving direct communication from God. In the Islamic understanding of prophet hood, the f i r s t man of the earth, Adam, was a Prophet and a Caliph. In the Qur'an, Dawood (David) is referred to as the Caliph (Q.38 : 26). In one tradition narrated from the Prophet, he is recorded to have said,

Kaanat banu Israael tasusu Anbiyaa 'a Kullama halaka Nabiyyun, Khalafa nabiyyun

---

[383] Scholars show that prophets were no mere prognosticators. They were spokesmen of a living Word from God. Their reference to their future resulted from their spiritual importance and moral urgency of the present. See, for Hebrew Prophets, R.B.Y. Scott, *The Relevance of The Prophets*, pp.1-18.

(In the Children of Israel was the foundation of Prophet hood. Each time a Prophet died, a Successor Prophet was appointed.)

Based on this, Muslims believe that the last Prophet from the Children of Israel is `Isa ibn Maryam (Jesus, Son of Mary), who was next to last in the continuous chain of prophet hood that began with Adam. Muslims believe that after him, the last of all prophets was Muhammad. Islam further holds that all these prophets were Caliphs as well as prophets.

With prophecy coming to an end with Muhammad, in the belief of Islam, the caliphate passed on to be collective in the hands of the *Umma*. It is perhaps for this reason, as we stated earlier, that when Abu Bakr became the Caliph, he used as a title, not simply "a caliph" but specifically "Khalifat Rasul Allah", i.e. "successor of the Messenger of Allah". When his successor, Umar, became a Caliph, he used the title "Successor of the Successor of the Messenger of Allah". Only when the title was becoming cumbersome, was it shortened to Khalifa. Theologians can argue that just as the history of the Caliphate went through the process of evolution, the history of humankind as a whole went through evolution as well. From the Cavemen, mankind moved to the tribal system. When tribes came to live together, society evolved into a city-state and then into empires. The final stage of this would be the French and American revolutions when mankind developed to accept democratic principles. Thus the sovereignty that belonged to an emperor was transferred through the long process of evolution and then revolution into what it is today.

Likewise, it seems to me, Iqbal perhaps had in mind a process of evolution in the institution of Caliphate. The direct Caliphate ended with the last Prophet and moved on in the hands of those who accept the principle of vicegerency of God on the earth. If this is so, then Iqbal's thinking in his famous Allahabad address of 1930 makes sense when he asked Muslims in India to demand a state of their own—a state that would replace an individual Caliph and be represented by a

189

collective Caliphate through the process of ijtihad in a collective assembly.

We cannot know for sure exactly what Iqbal's innermost thoughts were. But in the circumstances we have sketched, it is sensible to conclude just as the social evolution forced the single human sovereign-emperor to be replaced by democratic institutions, so the institution of the Caliphate could profitably change in another direction. A one-man Caliph in the Ottoman empire could give way to a popular Caliphate.

Looked at in this light, this was the greatest contribution the Khilafat movement achieved.

BIBLIOGRAPHY

Sources in English Language
Articles, Books, Pamphlets and Unpublished Material

Abbas, M.H. *All About Khilafat.* Calcutta: Ray and Roychaudhury, 1923.

Afzal, Raf ique. *Selected Speeches and Statements of* the Quaid-i-*Azam Muhammad Ali Jinnah.* Lahore: Lahore research Society of Pakistan, University of the Punjab Publishers, 1966.

Ahmad, A z i z. Studies *in Islamic Culture in the Indian Environment.* London: Oxford University Press, 1964.

—. *Islamic Modernism in India and Pakistan.* London: Oxford University Press, 1967.

—___.—"Sayyid Ahmad Khan, Jam1 al-Din Afghani and Muslim Indiaw Studica *Islamica* (1960), pp.

Ahmad, Jamil-ud-Din. *Early Phase* of *Muslim Political Movemen.* Lahore: Publishers United Ltd.,1967, 13: pp.55-78.

Ahmad, N. *Muslin Separatism in British India: A Retrospective Study.* Lahore: Ferozsons Publications, 1991.

Ali, Muhammad. My *Life: A Fragment.* Afzal Iqbal, *ed.* Lahore: S.M. Ashraf, 1946.

—. *Thoughts of the Present Discontent.* Bombay: Bombay *Gazette* Press, 1907.

—. *Selected Writings and Speeches of Maulana Muhammad Ali.* Afzal Iqbal, ed. 2 vols. 2d. ed. Lahore: S.M. Ashraf, 1963.

Ali, Muhammad and Shaukat Ali. *Freedom of Faith and Its Price.* London: n. pub., 1920.

———. *For* India and Islam. Calcutta: Saraswati Library, 1922.

Allana, G. Pakistan Movement: *Historic Documents.* Lahore : Paradise Subscription Agency, 1968.

Armatrong, Karen. *Muhammad: A Biography of The Prophet*

Arnold, Thomas W. *The Caliphate.* 2nd ed. London: Routledge and Keegan Paul, 1965.

Ayoub, Mahmoud. *Redemptive Suffering in Islam: A Study of the Devotional Aspects of 'Ashura in Twel ver Shi 'i s m.* The Hague Mouton Publishers, 1978.

Aziz, K.K. *The Indian Khilafat Movement 1915-1933: A Documentary Record.* Karachi: Pak Publishers Limited, 1972.

—. *The Making of Pakistan: A Study in Nationalism.* London: Chatto & Windus, 1967.

Azad, Abul Kalam. *India Wins Freedom.* Bombay: Orient Longmans, 1959.

———. *Khilafat and Jazirat al-Arab.* Mirza Abdul *Qadir* Beg, tr. Bombay: Central Khilafat Comitee, 1920.

———. *Presidential Address at the Special Session of the Congress, Delhi, Septmber 13, 1923.* Aligarh: Jamia Millia Press, 1923.

————. *The Tarjuman al Qur'an,* Syed Abdul Latif, tr., 2 vols. Bombay: Asia Publishing House, 1962-67.

Bamford, P. C. *Histories of the Non-cooperation and Khilafat Movements.* Delhi: Government of India, 1925.

Barrier, *N.* Gerald. *Banned: Controversial Li tera ture and Political Control in British* India, 197-1947. Columbia:University of Missouri Press, 1974.

Bashier, Zakaria. *Sunshine at Madinah.* Leicester : The Islamic Foundation, 1990/1410 A.H.

Bhatnagar, S.K. *History of M.A.O. College, Aligarh.* Bombay: Asia Publishing House,1969.

Blunt, Wilfrid Scawen. *The Future of Islam.* London: Routledge and Kegan Paul, 1882.

Brailsford, Henry Noel. *Subject India.* London: Gollancz, 1943.

Brown, Norman. *The United States and India and Pakistan, Bangladesh.* Cambridge: Massachssettes, 1972.

Craddock, Reginald. *Dilenmra* in India. London: Constable & Co. Ltd. 1929.

Dale, Stephen F. "The Islamic Frontier in Southwest India: The Shahid as a Cultural Ideal among the Mapillas of Malabar." *Modern Asian Studies* (February, l977), 11: pp.41-55.

Desai, Mahadeo. *Maulana Abul Kalam Azad.* Agra : Shivalal Agarwala& Co., 1946.

Enayat, Hamid. *Modem Islamic Political Thought.* Austin: University of Texas Press, 1982.

Esposito, John L. *Islam: The straight Path.* New York: Oxford University Press, 2011.

Faruqui, Ziaul Hasan. *The Deoband School and Demand for Pakistan.* Bombay: Asia Publishing House, 1963.

Fredunberg, Mirza Kalichbeg, *The Chachnamah: An Ancient History of Sind.*

Friedman, Yohanan, Shaykh *Ahmad Sirhindi: An Outline of his Thought and a Study of His Image in the eyes of Posterity.* Montreal: McGill University Institute of Islamic Studies, 1971.

Gandhi, M. K. *"The Khilafat Question" Pamphlets in Young India 1919-1922.* New York: B.W. Heubson, 1923.

Gibb, Hamilton A. R. ed. Stanford, J. Shaw and William R. Polk. *Studies* in *Civilization of Islam.* Toronto: S. J. Reginald Saunders and Co., 1962

Hayat, Sikandar. *Aspects* of *Pakistan Movement.* Lahore : Progressive Publishers, 1991.

—. "Syed Ahmed Khan and the Foundation of Muslim Sepatatist Political Movement in India". *Pakistan Journal of Social Sciences,* 8 : 1-2 (Jan-July-Dec. 1482). pp.33-48.

Hanioglu, Sukru. *The Young Turks in Opposition.* New York: Oxford University Press, 1995.

Husain, Ashfaq, *The Quintessence of Islam: A Summary of the Commentary of Maulana Abul Kalam Azad on al-Fateha, the First Chapter of the Quran.* Bombay: New York Asia Publishing House, 1960.

Hourani, Albert. Arabic *Thought in Liberal Age 1798-1939.* London:Oxford University Press, 1967.

Ikram, Shaikh Muhamrnad. Modern *Muslim India and Birth of Pakistan.* Lahore: S.M. Ashraf, 1970.

Iqbal, Muhammad. *The Reconstruction* of *Religious Thought in Islam.* 2nd. ed., Lahore: M. Ashraf, 1982.

Jafri, S. H. M. *The Origins and Early Development of* Shi 'a *Islam.* London : Longman, 19 7 9.

Jalal, Ayesha. *The Sale Spokesman: Jinnah, The Muslim League and the Demand for Pakistan.* Cambridge : Cambridge University Press, 1985,

Jordens, J. T. F. *Swami Shraddhananada: His Life and Causes.* Delhi, Oxford University Press, 1981.

Keddie, Nikki R. *An Islamic Response to Imperialism: Political and Religious Writings of Jamal* al-*Din al-Afghani.* Los Angeles University of California Press, 1968.

Kennedy, Joseph. *Asian Nationalism in Twentieth Century.* London, Murray McMillan, 1968.

Khaliquzzaman, Chaudhry. *Pathway to Pakistan.* Lahore : Longmans Green, 1961.

Khan, Ahmad Sir Sayyid. *The Present State of Indian Politics.* Allahabad: Pioneer Press, 1888.

Khimjee, Husein. *The Attributes of God in the Monotheistic Faiths of Judeo-Christian and Islamic Traditions.* Bloomington: iUniverse,2011.

Kidwai, Shaikh Mushir Husain. "Islam and Nationalism" in *Muslim Review.* (London), (July-August 1919), pp.249-253.

Lelyweld, David. *Aligarh s First Generation : Muslim Solidarity in British India.* Princeton: Princeton University Press, 1978.

Lewis, Bernard. *The Emergence of Modern Turkey.* London: Oxford University Press, 1961.

Lyall, Sir Alfred. *Asiatic Studies:* Religious and Social. London: Murray McMillan, 1884.

Mahmud, Syed. The *Khilafat* and *England. Patna:* Mohemed Imtyaz, 1921.

Malik, Hafeez. *Sir Sayyid Ahmed Khan and Muslim Modernisation in India and Pakistan.* Columbia University *press,* 1980.

———. *Moslem Nationalism inIndia and Pakistan.* Washington : Public Affairs Press, 1963.

al-Mawardi, Abu al-Hasan Ali ibn Muhammad. *Al-Ahkam Al-Sultaniyah.* Cairo: *1881.*

Malik, Rizwan. *Mawlana Husayn Ahmad Madani and Jami* `yat-i *Ulama-I Hind 1920-1957: Status of Islam and Muslims in India.* Thesis, University of Toronto, 1995.

Mawdudi, Abu `1 A'ala. *Nationalism and India.* Pathankot: 1943

McLeod, W.H. *Who is a Sikh?* Oxford: Clarendon Press, 1989.

Metcalf, Barbara Daly. *Islamic Revival in British India: Deoband, 1860-1900.* Princeton: Princeton University Press, 1982.

Minault, Gail. *The Khilafat Movement: Religious Symbolism and Political Mobilisation in India.* New York: Columbia University Press, 1982.

Morrison, Theodore. "England *and* Islam" *Nineteenth Century.* (June 1919), 86 : 116-122.

Mujahid, Sharif. nComrmnal Riots." *A History of Freedom Movements* Vol. IV part 11. Karachi: Pakistan Historical Society, 1960.

Mujahid, N. *Quaid-i-Azam Jinnah: Studies in Interpretation.* Karachi: Quaid-i-Azam Academy, 1981.

Mujeeb, M. *The Indian Muslims.* London: Allan and Unwin, 1967.

—. *Maulana Abul Kalam Arad: A Memorial Volume.* Bombay: Asia Publishing House, 1959.

Naim, C.M. *Iqbal, Jinnah and Pakistan: The Vision and Reality.* Lahore: Vanguard Books, 1984.

Nehru, Jawaharlal, *An Autobiography.* Delhi : Allied Publishers, 1962.

Niemeijer, A.C. The *Khilafat Movement in India, 1919-1924.* The Hague : Martinius Nijhoff, 1972.

O'Dwyer Michael. *India as I Knew It 1885-1925.* London: Constable, 1925.

Pirzada, S. *Quaid-i-Azm Jinnah 's Correspondence.* Karachi : East and West Publishing Co., 1977.

Powell, Baden Henry. *A Short Account of the Land Revenue in India.* Oxford: Oxford University Press, 1984.

Qureshi, N. "Jinnah and Khilafat Movement 1918-1923" *Journal of South Asian and Middle Eastern Studies* Vols. 1-2. (December,1977), pp. 82-107.

Ramsaur, Ernest Edrnondson. *The Young Turks: Prelude to the Revolution of 1908.* Princeton: Princeton University Press, 1957.

al-Razi, al-Imam al-Fakhr. *al-Tafsir al-Kabir.* Beirut: n.pub., n.d.

Rosenthal, Erwin I. J. *Political Thought in Medieval Islam.* Cambridge : Cambridge University Press, 1962.

Sarkar Jagaxmath, A.B. Bardhan and N. E. Balram, *India 's Freedom Struggle: Several Streams.* New Delhi : Peoples Publishing House,1986.

Scott, R.B.Y. *The Relevance of the Prophets.* New York: Oxford University Press, 1957.

Sen, Sachin. *The Birth of Pakistan.* Calcutta: Calcutta General Printers and Publishers, 1955.

Shaikh, Farzana. *Community and Consensus in Islam: Muslim Representation in Colonial India, 1860-1947.* Cambridge : Cambridge University Press, 1989.

Shamool. *Speeches, Writings and Statements of Iqbal.* Lahore : al-Mana Academy, 1948.

Shan, Muhammad. *Freedom Movement in India: The Role of Ali Brothers.* New Delhi: Associate Press, 1979.

Smith, Wilfred Cantwell. *Islam in Modern History.* Princeton: Princeton University Press, 1957.

—. *Modem* Islam in India, London: Victor Gollancz, 1946.

Suyuti, A. *History of the Caliphs.* tr., H.S. Javed. Calcutta: Asiatic Society, 1881.

Syed, Anwar H. "Iqbal and Jinnah on issues of Nationhood and Nationalism" *Iqbal, Jinnah and Pakistan: The Vision and Reality. Lahore:* Vanguard Books, 1984.

Tendulkar, D.G. *Mahatma.* 2 vols. Delhi: Govt. of India Publications Division, 1957.

Thompson, Edward and G.T. Garratt. *Rise and Fulfilment of British Rule in India.* Allahabad: Central Book Depot, 1962.

Toynbee, A.J., "Trial of the Leaders at Karachi" *Modern Review.* (Calcutta), (December 1921), 30 (6). pp.755-756.

—. "Relation between British India, Soviet Russia and Afghanistan, 1919-1923." *Survey of International Affairs 1920-1923.*

Thursby, G. R. *Hindu-Muslim Relations in British India.* Leiden: B r i l l, 1975.

Vahid, S.A. *Studies in Iqbal.* Lahore: M. Ashraf, 1967.

Von Gruenbaum, G. E. *Muslim Self-Statement in India and Pakistan.* Wiesbaaden:1970.

Watson, *J.W. Muhammad Ali and the Khilafat Movement.* Thesis, M.A., M c G i l l University, 1976.

Williams, Rushbrook L.F. *The State of Pakistan.* London: 1962.

Yate Asadullah. *Al-Ahkam al-Sul taniyyah* (The Laws of Islamic Governance). London: Ta-ha Publishers, 1996.

Proscribed Material

Caliphs of Islam
Ci vi1 disobedience movemen t
Communal conflicts
Communal unity
Comrade : *supplements*
Hindu domination in India
History of the Hindu-Muslim problemin India

Indian poli tical prisoners
Islamic fra terni ty
Kanpur Mosque
Khilafat movement
Khilafat movement—importance for *Muslims*
Khilafat and non-cooperation movements
Nationalist Muslims
Ruin of *India by British rule*
Struggle for *the Swarajya*
'ulamaf advocate communal unity

Newspapers, Chronicles and Journals

Bombay Chronicle
Independent
Modem Review
Nineteenth Century
Tribune
Islamic Culture

Articles, Books, Pamphlets. and Unpublished Material

Ahmed, Habib. *Tehrik-i Pakistan.* n. pub., n.d.

Ali, Muhammad. *Majmua-i-Kalam-i-Jauhar.* Delhi : Delhi Publishing Works, 1918.

———. *Kalam-i*-Jauhar. Delhi: Kutub Khana-i-Naziriya, n. d.

.-..—T-aq-ar iren *Maulana Muhammad Ali.* 2 vols., Lucknow: Ghani Press, 1921.

Azad, Abul Kalam. *Masala-i-Khilafat wa Jazirat al-Arab.* Calcutta: Al-Balagh Press, 1920.

—. *Khutba t-i-Sadarat Taqriri.* Delhi : Swaraj PublishingWorks, 1921.

———. Maulana *Abul Kalam* Azad ka Paigham. Delhi: Swaraj Publishing Works, 1922.

—. Talimi *Tark-i Mawalat ka Maqsad.* Delhi: Swaraj Publishing Works, n.d.

—. *Tazkira.* Malik Ram, ed. 26. ed., Delhi: Sahitya Academy, 1968.

—. *Azad ki Kahani khud Azad ki Zubani.* As dictated to Abdul Razaq Malehabadi, Delhi: Maktaba-i-Ishaiyat al-Quran, 1965.

Bari, Abdul. "Masala-i Khilafat wa Darul Islam." *AL-Nizamiyya* (Feb. 1919), 4 (12) 1-7.

—. *Fitna-i-1rtidad aur Musalmanon ka Fan.* Lucknow: Fitangi Mahal, 1922 (1341 A.H.).

—.—*Ul-am.a-i-*Hind *ka Fatwa Masala-i-Khilafat par.* Lucknow: Al-Nazir Press, 1920.

ibn Basyuni Zaghlul, *Musnad al-*Imam *Ahmed ibn Hanbal. Dar al-*Kitab al-'Ilmiyya, Beirut: 1989, vol. 4, p.273.

Choudhury, Habib Ahmad. *Tehrik-i Pakistan aur Neshnalist Ulama*

Dariyabadi, Abdul Majid. "Jauhar aur unki Shairi" *Kal am-i-Jauhar.* Delhi: Kutubkhana-i-Nazari~a, n.d., 1-23.

———. *Malbar wa Muplah. Kanpur:* Daftar-1-Daairat-i-Ilmiyya, 1923.

Hall, Maulana Altaf Husain. *Hayat-idavid.* Lahore: n. pub., 1957.

Inayatullah, M. *Hasrat al-Afaq ba Vafat-i-Majmua al-Akhlaq.* Lucknow: Firangi Mahal, 1929.

Madani, Husain Ahmad. *Naqsh-i Hayat.* 2 vols., Deoband: Maktabai-Diniyya, 1953.

———. *Dastur-i-Asasi-i Jamiat-i-Khilafat-i Hind.* Bombay: Central Khilafat Committee, n.d.

Miyan, M. *Jamiatul Ulama Kya Hai.* 2 vols., Delhi : Jamiatul Ulama, 1946.

__,_-_. *Ul ma-i-Haq aur Unke M jahidana Karname.* Delhi : n. pub., n.d.

Nadwi, Abdul Hasanat. *Khilafat-i-Islamiyya aur Turk.* Delhi: n.pub. 1920 (1339 A.H.).

Nadwi, Sayyid Sulayman. *Dunya-i-Islam aur Masala-i-Khilafat.* Bombay : Khilaf at Press, 1921.

Narang, Gopi Chand. *Sakh-i-Karbala Betwur-i Shairi Istiara t Urdu Shairi ka ek Takhlliqi Rujhan.* New Delhi: Shastri Indo-Canadian Institute, 1986.

Qureshi, Wahid. *Pakistan ki Nazariati Bunyaden.* Lahore : Educational Emporium, 1973.

Rizvi, Sayyid Mahbub. *Tarikh-i-Dewband.* Deoband : Idara-i Tarikh-i-Deoband, 1952.

Shafi, M. *Afdalat-i Ashrafiyah dar Masail-i Siyasiyah.* Deoband : Dar al-Isha'at, 1945.

Thanawi, Ashraf Ali. *Khatab ba Muslim Lig.* Sharanpur: Majlis Da'awat al-Haq, 1938.

—. *Taimir-i Pakistan* aur *Ulama-i Rabbani.*

Websites

www.archive.org/stream/khilafatengland00mahm/ khilafatengland00mahm_djvu.txt.

www.scribd.com/doc/80754308/.

www.archive.org/stream/historyofindiann00loveuoft/ historyofindiann00loveuoft_djvu.txt.

www.oocities.org/mubarak4one/mubarak/khilafat.htm.

www.amazon.it/The-Khilafat-England-Classic-Reprint/ dp/B008N6H3TO www.scribd.com/doc/39243063/ Jinnah-Khilafat-and-RSS.

www.scribd.com/doc/100495764/The-Emergence-of-Ulema-in-the-Politics-of-India-and-Pakistan-1918-1949.

www.scribd.com/doc/80754308/The-Caliphate-Question-The-British-Government-and-Islamic-Governance.

www.brecorder.com/supplements/88/1166817/.

www.britannica.com/EBchecked/topic/285905/Indian-philosophy/ 12370

www.scribd.com/doc/102239725/5/,

www.rebuildpakistan.net and "Quaid e Azam Mohammad Ali Jinnah", in http://az-mohaljinnah.blogspot.com/

www.archive.org/stream/speechesandwriti032213mbp/ speechesandwriti032213mb p_djvu.txt

Proscribed Material

Azadi ke Sahida
Baikat
Bambai ka Khuni Muharram
Dard-i Khilafat
Dard-i vatan
Difans-i Islam
Durr-i Muhammadi
Fatva *tark-i muvalat*
Hartala
Hindus tan-men Angrezi Ra j
Hindustan men Angrezo sen jang karneka yeh-i vaqt hai
*Jihan-*i *Islam*
Kangresa membaron se apila
Kanpur ki Khuni dastan
Khutba-yi Sadarat aur fatva *tark-i muvalat*
Mazalumon ki aha
Muttahidah qaumiyyat aur *Islam*
Tarikh-i Shi 'ah
Yadgar-i Karbala
Zul aqar-i Haidari
Zul faqar-i Saf dari

Newspapers, Journals and Chronicles

al-Balagh
al-Hilal
Hamdard
Inquilab
Pai gham
Nawa-i-Waqt

INDEX